The

Fascinating History of American Indians

The Age Before Columbus

Tim McNeese

Enslow Publishers, Inc.
40 Industrial Road
Box 398
Berkeley Heights, NJ 07922
USA
        http://www.enslow.com

America's
Living History

Library of Congress Cataloging-in-Publication Data:

McNeese, Tim.

The fascinating history of American Indians: the age before Columbus / Tim McNeese.

p. cm.—(America's living history)

Summary: "Examines the history of American Indians before the arrival of Christopher Columbus and other European explorers to North America"—Provided by publisher.

Includes bibliographical references and index.

ISBN-13: 978-0-7660-2938-5

ISBN-10: 0-7660-2938-7

1. Paleo-Indians—Juvenile literature. 2. Indians—Origin—Juvenile literature. 3. North America—Antiquities—Juvenile literature. I. Title.

E61.M48 2009

970.1—dc22

2007044924

Printed in the United States of America

10 9 8 7 6 5 4 3 2 1

Illustration Credits: Associated Press, pp. 11, 18, 34; The Bridgeman Art Library, p. 77; © Corel Corporation, p. 45; Courtesy of the Division of Anthropology, American Museum of Natural History [50/6509], p. 68 (inset); Enslow Publishers, Inc., pp. 24, 39; Gary Hincks/Science Photo Library, p. 23; The Granger Collection, New York, pp. 61, 64; © 2007 istock International Inc., Paul Senszyn, p. 26; Illustration by Joyce Bergen, © 1999, p. 4; © JupiterImages Corporation, pp. 68 (background), 70; Library of Congress, pp. 80 (men on horseback), 91, 103; Mary-Ella Keith/Alamy, p. 110; © North Wind/Nancy Carter/North Wind Picture Archives, pp. 43, 78; North Wind Picture Archives, p. 29; North Wind Picture Archives/Alamy, p. 88; Shutterstock.com, Armin Rose, p. 21; Shutterstock.com, Duncan Gilbert, p. 49; Shutterstock.com, Jason Cheever, p. 52; Shutterstock.com, John L. Richbourg, p. 59; Shutterstock.com, Jose Gil, p. 93; Shutterstock.com, Natalia Bratslavsky, p. 98; Shutterstock.com, SueC, p. 95; Werner Forman/Art Resource, NY, pp. 73, 80 (counting-coup stick).

Cover Illustration: The Granger Collection, New York (painting); Shutterstock.com, Natalia Bratslavsky (totem pole).

Cover Image Description: A portion of a painting by George Catlin of the Mandan Indian Bull Dance (background).

Contents

Scientists believe an ancient hunter who they call Kennewick Man once stalked his prey with only a spear as his weapon.

Chapter 1

An Ancient Hunter

Quietly, with all his senses focused on his objective, the hunter crouched as he stepped across the leafy ground, searching for tracks. His grip tightened around the smooth piece of wood he held in his right hand. The length of wood he held stood taller than he did. He had fashioned it with his own hands and worked it into a weapon that he hoped would serve him well this day. It lay balanced in his hand, almost as if it were a part of him, a natural extension of himself. The shaft represented life for him and death for others. He would use the wooden shaft as a weapon, and the animal he hoped to kill with it would provide him with food. Its skin would provide a covering for his body or protection for his feet.

It was not the wooden shaft that would actually deliver death to his animal victim, but the sharpened stone secured to its tip. The hunter had worked longer on the stone for his weapon than he had on the wooden shaft itself. For hours, he had sat cross-legged, concentrating on sharpening the stone that would turn the wooden stick into a tool of survival. First, he had struck off pieces of stone from a larger rock until he had broken off one with the general shape he needed to begin making the spearhead. Using a piece of antler as a tool, he had then carefully chipped at the edges of the stone. His skillful hands reworked the stone until it had a shape only a human could give it—symmetrical, balanced, identical on both of its flat sides. Once he achieved this, he began giving his stone a sharp edge. It would need to be sharp enough to pierce the tough hide of his animal prey. Steadying his rough, calloused hands, he chipped at the stone's edge. Finally, he tested the sharpened edge on his finger, leaving a small cut. It was ready. Using animal sinew, he had attached the spear tip to the wooden shaft. Wood and stone had become a lethal weapon.

He gingerly took another step, his leather-wrapped foot softly touching the forest floor. While he made no sound, he heard something and froze. A crack of a twig? A falling acorn? The quick dart of a ground squirrel? Had it come from his right? No, maybe ahead of him. He scanned the trees before him and the forest floor, crouching even lower. Everything before him was brown and silent again. His hand clenched the wooden shaft tighter even as he raised it next to his right ear. There, between those two trees in the distance ahead of him—a deer, perhaps? Almost in answer to his question, a step was taken. But this time, it was not his foot, but the thin, brown-skinned foreleg of his prey. The deer took a step as cautious as any the hunter had taken that day. The animal raised its head from the forest floor and sniffed the air. Its black eyes scanned between the trees for danger. But the breeze did not cooperate. The scent of the hunter remained elusive.

Silently, the hunter moved forward into better range. His spear was in position; his confused quarry in front of him. The hours of working wood and stone into a weapon would soon be worth it all. Before the hunter stood an animal that could become food and clothing. But the skills of the moment would be those of patience, stealth, muscle power, and accuracy. Slowly, the hunter took another step.

Then, a new sound, this one coming from his immediate right. A shadowy shape moved quickly toward him. His concentrated gaze moved from the deer, which had also heard the new sound and had responded with a bound in the opposite direction. He shifted his attention to his right, but his movements were a fraction of a second too late. Even as he focused his gaze on the shape moving toward him, he realized he had held his spear too long. It was not an animal, but another man, a stranger to him, another hunter. And this hunter had no spear in his hand. In less than a second, he understood why. He felt a sharp pain in his side as a piece of stone, one

similar to the stone he had shaped for his own spear, pierced his skin. The pain was sharp as the stone buried itself deep in his flesh, piercing his pelvic bone. As he fell to the ground, he dropped his own spear even as he reached for the spear that had struck him, a weapon delivered by the strong hand of an enemy. Struggling on the leafy forest floor, the hunter had become the victim.

Along the Banks of the Columbia

The story presented on the previous pages may not have happened exactly as described. But thousands of years ago, such a hunter did live and die. He might have died completely forgotten, except that his remains would surface in a most extraordinary way. On a warm, late July day in 1996, a pair of college students were engaged in one of their favorite activities—watching the local hydroplane races that took place annually along the Columbia River, the western-flowing waterway that separates southern Washington State from northern Oregon. That day, they walked along the banks of Lake Wallula, a portion of the Columbia River formed behind the McNary Dam, near the local town of Kennewick. This pair of boat-racing enthusiasts had come for the highly publicized event, not expecting the river to produce anything but an exciting spectator sport.[1]

As they waded through the water, they stirred up

the river bottom's silt and mud. They could not have known they were on the edge of creating an even greater stir, one that would begin as a mystery and end as a struggle among the government, local American Indian tribes, the U.S. Army Corps of Engineers, and the nation's courts. Suddenly, near the river's edge, in shallow water, the students saw something in the water that immediately drew them away from the racing event and into an arena of mystery. In the water, stuck in the mud and silt, the two young men saw a portion of a human skull.

Since the discovery of the bones was made in Benton County, Washington, the local coroner was called. He was interested in trying to establish the cause of death. Perhaps, someone had simply fallen into the river and drowned. There might have been some other sort of accident. But the coroner was also aware there might be a more sinister reason for the existence of the skull in the river. Perhaps it was a murder victim. Further examination along the river might reveal additional bones, possibly providing the coroner with more evidence.

But something was not right. An examination of the skull made it clear to the county official that he was not looking at something as simple as a boating mishap, river accident, or even a modern-day crime. The skull

and bones were not those of someone who had died recently.

Soon, the coroner called in someone who might be able to help him with the mysterious bones in the river. Jim Chatters was a local forensic anthropologist who worked for the Benton County sheriff's department. (A forensic anthropologist is a scientist who studies earlier humans and their ancestors.) His studies were based on scientific investigation and professional training. The slightly built, bearded Chatters was an expert in his field.[2]

Yes, the bones are old, Chatters assured the county coroner. He collected the bones and took them to his lab. Laying them out on an examination table, Chatters assembled the bones side by side, placing them in relation to one another. At the top of the table he laid the skull. Below the old head bone, he recreated a picture of the detached skeletal remains. His work along the river had produced dozens and dozens of bone parts from complete arm and leg bones to pieces of ribs, vertebrae, even finger and toe bones. In all, the skeletal remains he and the county coroner, Floyd Johnson, had removed from the river represented 90 percent of a complete skeleton, including all of its teeth. Only the sternum and a few small hand and feet bones were missing. There was much to examine. Although the person in question had not died recently, Chatters had almost everything

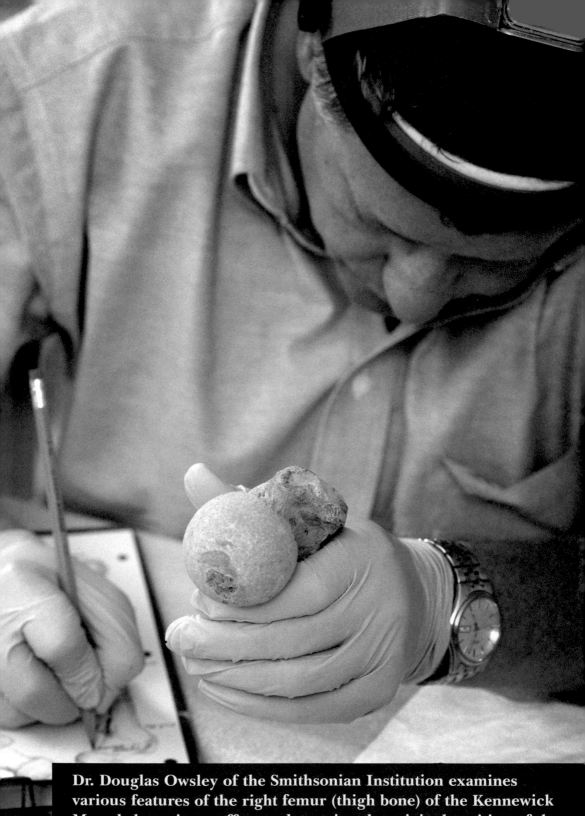

Dr. Douglas Owsley of the Smithsonian Institution examines various features of the right femur (thigh bone) of the Kennewick Man skeleton in an effort to determine the original position of the body in the ground.

in front of him that he needed to make an informed examination.[3]

Taking a close look at the skull, its dimensions, the position and size of the eye sockets, and the line of the jaw and cheek bones led Chatters to deduce that the skull's former owner had been a Caucasoid, someone whose race typically is identified as "white." Perhaps, Chatters then surmised, the bones had belonged to some long-forgotten frontier settler, an Anglo-American resident from the 1800s. Oregon had, after all, been a destination for hundreds of thousands of white Americans during the nineteenth century, many of whom had reached the region of the Columbia River by crossing the western United States. Had this unknown man fallen victim as a hapless member of a wagon party bound for the rich farming lands of what was once called "Oregon Country"?[4]

Chatters's assumption about the bones made immediate sense. But the anthropologist's theory did not remain intact for long. To learn more about the "victim," Chatters performed a CT scan, which produced a three-dimensional image of the bones and showed something that the forensic anthropologist had missed in his examination. He discovered a foreign object embedded in the skeleton's right pelvis, one that would have been unlikely in nineteenth-century Oregon—a Stone Age spear point.

The discovery blasted a large hole in Chatters's

theory. The projectile point was of gray stone, a leaf-shaped projectile point known as a Cascade. It was a variety that had likely not been in use in the nineteenth century. The curious forensic anthropologist then took the next obvious step. He had to know as precise a date for the bones as possible.

To this end, Chatters sent a small bit of finger bone to be examined at a second laboratory, one at the University of California, Riverside (UCR). There, scientists took the tiny finger bone fragment and ran a test designed to date older bones. The test was a type of radiocarbon dating, one commonly used by anthropologists to date carbon-based materials, such as hair and bones, to determine how old they might be. The test could tell Chatters whether the bones he had been examining dated to the nineteenth century or if they might be a little older.[5]

By the time the results came back from the UCR laboratory, a month had passed since the discovery of the bones in the Columbia River. The test results were immediately startling to Chatters. The bones did not date to the nineteenth century. They were old bones, alright. But no one could have predicted how old. The Caucasoidal man they had belonged to had once walked along the banks of the Columbia River more than nine thousand years ago![6]

A Controversial Discovery

The exciting discovery of a nine thousand-year-old American Indian skeleton sent a shock wave through the archaeological community. Only a few dozen skeletal remains that old had ever been excavated in the United States, and none of them were nearly as complete as the bones that would soon become known as Kennewick Man. But soon a new controversy emerged.

Just four days following the announcement of the dating of the bones, the United States government and others intervened. The U.S. Army Corps of Engineers ordered all scientific testing to cease and reclaimed possession of the skeleton. Since the bones were identified as thousands of years old, several local American Indian groups, including the Umatilla of Oregon and Washington, and the Nez Perce, Yakama, Wannapum, and Colville peoples claimed the skeleton.

Their claim rested on a federal law that was only six years old in 1996: the Native American Graves Protection and Repatriation Act (NAGPRA). When passed in 1990, the act served to protect American Indian artifacts and remains, such as an ancient skeleton, from being excavated and removed from their original sites. Indians who could "show by a preponderance of archaeological, geological, historical, or other evidence that they have some cultural affiliation"[7] to a specific artifact or human remains could take possession of such items as part of their tribal heritage. Once the American Indian claim was made to have Kennewick Man returned to modern-day Indians for reburial, the U.S. Army Corps of Engineers intervened on their behalf. (The Corps would later choose to bulldoze the site where the skeletal remains had been discovered, an extremely controversial step.)

Suddenly, scientists interested in studying the fascinating collection of nine thousand-year-old bones discovered in the Columbia River saw their opportunity slipping away. By October 17, almost three months after the discovery of the bones, eight American anthropologists, including those with the Smithsonian Institution, sued for their right to study the bones. The case, *Bonnichsen* et al. v. *The United States of America*, soon placed various groups against one another. National Park Service (NPS) officials were asked to help settle the struggle between the American Indians and the scientists. After an examination of the bones, the NPS decided in favor of repatriation of the skeleton to the Umatilla. However, a federal district court agreed with the anthropologists. As the case advanced further, a circuit court agreed with the lower court, "citing a lack of cultural and genetic evidence to link the bones to the [Umatilla]."[8]

But Kennewick Man's legal status continued to be unclear and undecided for years. During those years, the bones remained in limbo. Various government entities vied against one another. But after conflicting rulings, orders, and decisions by the Army Corps of Engineers, the Department of the Interior, the Clinton administration, and, ultimately, the courts, Kennewick Man's fate was determined. On February 4, 2004, the U.S. Court of Appeals for the Ninth Circuit rejected all tribal claims to the skeleton, ruling that no group could show evidence of kinship. Also, the court decided the remains could be examined by scientists interested in discovering what the ancient bones might be able to tell modern humans about at least one of their early ancestors.[9]

Some facts were simple. Kennewick Man, when he lived during the Pleistocene Era, stood approximately five feet nine inches tall. He was a fit and muscular individual. He was right-handed and had arthritis in his right elbow, both his knees, and several of his spinal vertebrae. As to his age at death, earlier estimates put it at forty-five to fifty-five, but researchers later lowered their conclusion to as young as thirty-eight. He had probably spent a lifetime hunting and had experienced serious injury more than once. At some time, he had broken an arm. According to forensic anthropologist Douglas Owsley, with the Smithsonian Institution's National Museum of Natural History: "One rib was fractured and healed and there is a depression fracture on his forehead and similar indentation on the left side of the head."[10] Owsley reported that even the spear wound was not fatal, since the pelvic site appears to have healed.

As to the earlier suggestion that Kennewick Man appeared "Caucasoidal," even Chatters would eventually back off from that claim. According to Chatters:

> I tried . . . to curtail that business about Caucasians in America early . . . [Kennewick Man] is not North American looking, and he's not tied in to Siberian or Northeast Asian populations. He looks more Polynesian or more like the Ainu [an ethnic group that is now found only in northern Japan but in prehistoric times lived throughout coastal areas of eastern Asia] or southern Asians.[11]

Even though the site where Kennewick Man had been discovered had been covered over by the Army Corps of Engineers, scientists concluded that he had been buried. They based their conclusion on the high level of calcium carbonate deposits found on the underside of the bones, indicating "he was lying on his back with his feet rolled slightly outward and his arms at his side, the palms facing down—a position that could hardly have come about by accident."[12] (There was also no

evidence that the body had been scavenged by wild animals, so it likely was not above ground.) The scientists also gave an answer as to how the bones had remained undetected for thousands of years only to be discovered in shallow waters near the banks of the Columbia. Their conclusion: Kennewick Man's body had been buried parallel to the river and the site had only been exposed through river erosion. The evidence suggests that the bones may have only been unearthed between six months to a year before discovery. This would also explain why so many of the bones were discovered so closely together. Exposure over a long period would have dispersed the bones over a much greater area.[13]

More than a decade has passed since the discovery of ancient American bones along the banks of the

A clay model of the head of Kennewick Man, based on his nine-thousand year-old skull, is shown at Columbia Basin College in Richland, Washington. The likeness was made by sculptor Tom McClelland and anthropologist Jim Chatters.

Columbia River. The remains are currently housed at the Burke Museum at the University of Washington, where they have been since October 1998. However, the U.S. Army Corps of Engineers legally owns the bones, since the skeletal remains were first discovered on land owned by the Corps.

Studies of Kennewick Man continue. What additional secrets the bones still may yield remains unknown. But the existence of Kennewick Man—an early resident of the Western Hemisphere—suggests other questions: Who was he really? From where did he or his predecessors come? How did he live? How did he die? What was life like for those early inhabitants of the Americas? Many of these questions may never be fully answered for the mysterious man who lived along the Pacific Coast more than nine millennium ago. But modern-day scientists, anthropologists, and archaeologists continue to search for new clues to uncover more evidence. They wish to reveal pasts lived long ago—lives that formed the world of America's first people.

Chapter 2

America's First People

There are many theories concerning the earliest arrivals to North America. Sometimes these theories agree with one another; sometimes they do not. While different scientists, anthropologists, and even historians may disagree on which theory is the most likely, they do agree in general on some of the details. However else others might have found their way to the Americas over thousands of years, many arrived by walking from Siberia, the frozen reaches of modern-day Russia, to the New World by a land bridge.

As recently as five hundred years ago, the existence of the two entire continents now called North America and South America was not recognized in Europe. While ancient peoples, many thousands of years ago, did migrate to North and South America, the connections between Asia and the Western Hemisphere had long been severed by 1500. (The term Western Hemisphere refers to the lands that comprise the Americas, including North,

South, and Central America and the islands that dot the Caribbean Sea.) The peoples outside the Americas were unaware of its size, the scope and lay of the land, or of the tens of millions of people who had made their homes on its plains, along its valleys, up on its hills and mountains, and along its rivers and lakes. The world of the Americas was virtually unknown in the other half of the world.

Global Cooling

Prior to the arrival of the first humans in the Americas, the world experienced a series of periods of cold that scientists today call ice ages. During such periods, when the temperature of the planet is colder for a long period of time, the ice of the polar north extended further south. This happened because the earth was experiencing "global cooling." This caused more of the world's water supply to become locked in the form of ice, rather than as a liquid or a vapor, such as steam. In turn, with more water taking the form of ice, the level of the earth's seas and oceans dropped. As the sea levels lowered, greater amounts of land that had been underwater were exposed above water. This natural phenomenon, the cooling of the planet and the increasing of the earth's polar ice, was an important period of change. All this relates to the process of how the first humans arrived in North America.[1]

However, the plains, mountains, lakes, and rivers were not in the same form as when the first peoples of the Americas lived on the land. During prehistoric times, the landscape of the Americas, especially North America, was different from what it is today.[2]

Most scientists, including anthropologists and archaeologists (people who attempt to recover the past by digging up artifacts, or ancient items, left behind by earlier peoples), believe the first humans may have migrated to America during one or both of the two most recent ice ages. During these periods, with more land exposed by low sea levels, the landmass that normally separated North America from the farthest, eastern reaches of Asia was exposed above water. Anthropologists refer to the most recent ice age as the Pleistocene Era. This era took place from around 1.8 million to about ten thousand years ago.[3]

During the Pleistocene Era, immense, massive glaciers stood thousands of feet above the landscape as giant ice mountains. These huge glaciers held so much water that sea levels may have dropped as much as three hundred feet lower than they are today. The land normally submerged underwater, between Asia and North America, a waterway today known as the Bering Strait, would have been above sea level. Because of this, a large piece of open land extending many miles north and south was opened. Today, the name given to this temporary stretch of exposed land is Beringia. The land was ice-free and thick with lush grasses. These formed a large meadow or pasture for animals who migrated into the region. Unlike the climate in that part of the world today, it would have been somewhat warmer in summer and dry and cold in winter.[4]

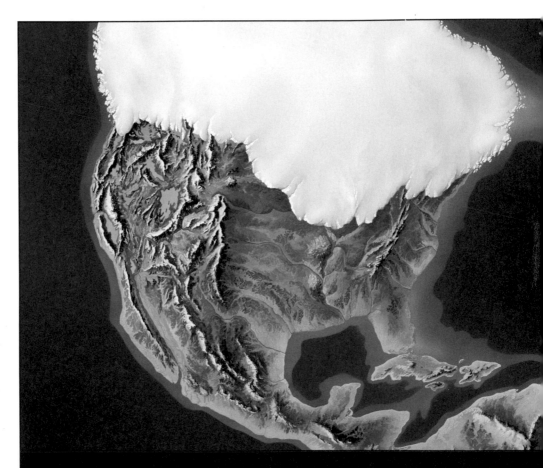

During the Pleistocene Era, the Arctic ice extended far into North America. The ice was almost a mile deep. To the south, the cooling produced mountain glaciers, enormous lakes, and a lowered sea level.

It was here that ice age mammals migrated, fed, and roamed about. These included Pleistocene horses, camels, reindeer, and bison. The horses were much smaller than modern horses and the bison were massive compared with today's shaggy beasts. The early camels would serve as the ancestors of modern-day llamas found in South America. The animals shared company with others, including musk oxen, saber-toothed tigers, and beavers as large as bears.

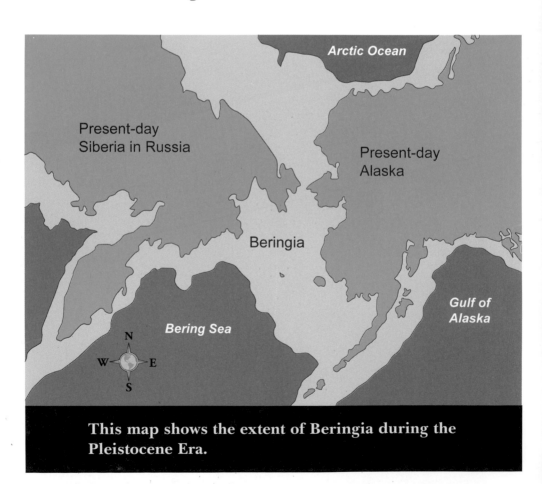

This map shows the extent of Beringia during the Pleistocene Era.

But above all these Pleistocene Era beasts stood creatures of enormous size—mastodons and woolly mammoths. As the name implies, mammoths were immense. (They were actually larger than today's elephants!) They lived until the end of the Pleistocene Era, around ten thousand years ago. Mammoths towered over every other land animal at ten feet in height. Mastodons were nearly as large, but covered with a thick shaggy coat of hair. Unlike the mammoths, mastodons had over-sized, long, curved tusks. Just as the mammoths did before them, the mastodons went extinct in North America.[5]

As the lush grasses of Beringia lured all these animals, large and small alike, out of the continent of modern-day Asia, they continued to migrate over Beringia and into the Western Hemisphere. Ancient humans in Asia who hunted the animals for food followed them. Other animals migrated out of America to the Eastern Hemisphere.

When the last ice age ended, about ten thousand years ago, the sea levels rose once more, leaving Beringia as it had been before—covered with water. This left the animals and the people who had reached the Western Hemisphere as permanent residents of this new land. They continued to hunt and spread out across the landscape of their new continent. In time, the large Pleistocene animals went extinct. No longer did great

mammoths tower above the land. The giant beavers, the tiny horses—they all passed out of existence, leaving only their bones to be found by modern archaeologists, anthropologists, and paleontologists. As for the people—perhaps the first to reach the Americas—they settled in to meet the challenges of living in their new environment as the continent's first "Americans."[6]

Woolly mammoth skeletons are still found in the United States today.

Crafters of Stone

Today, scientists still know little about the origins of the first humans in the Western Hemisphere. That they came to these unknown lands as migratory hunters seems indisputable. They certainly would have been here as early as twelve thousand to fifteen thousand years ago. But some anthropologists and paleontologists believe the first humans in the Americas reached the continent much earlier than that. True, the most recent ice age ended about ten thousand years ago, but another ice age occurred before that era. That earlier ice age lasted several thousand years.[7]

But, simply because an earlier ice age took place does not guarantee that people arrived in the Western Hemisphere during that time. Scientists need evidence to make such a claim. A few sites that have been excavated over the past few decades may point to human life in the Americas prior to ten thousand years ago. Discoveries made during recent years in two locations—Daisy Cave in California and Monte Verde, Chile—indicate that groups of people, Asians probably, moved down the Pacific coast of North and South America during a much earlier period of human occupation. Some archaeologists place those coastal migrations as early as 30,000 B.C.[8] The Monte Verde site in Chile may be older than 30,000 B.C. Radiocarbon testing has been done on the site.

The earliest such date proving human occupation at Monte Verde is some twelve thousand five hundred years ago.[9]

But controversy continues to dog these sites. The problem lies in the evidence itself. Although anthropologists have worked hard at these locations and found such evidence as bones and stone objects, questions remain. Determining whether a stone or bone artifact was actually worked by a human being is sometimes difficult to establish. Therefore, these sites in western Canada's Yukon, California, Chile, and elsewhere remain under scrutiny. As a result, the safest dating of humans in America is about fifteen thousand years ago.

Tools and Weapons

What kind of people were these first travelers who crossed Beringia into the Western Hemisphere? A lack of evidence makes it difficult to know and understand the first people in the Americas. It also makes it difficult to pinpoint a time or date by which they arrived. Most scientists believe that the first people who wandered across the great Bering land bridge thousands of years ago were following the migratory animals of the Pleistocene Era. They hunted these animals for clothing and food.

These early groups of hunter-gatherers were constantly on the move, following the animals as they migrated from place to place. These ancient peoples were nomadic, meaning they did not remain settled in a single place for long, since they followed the footsteps of the migrating animals. As the animal herds moved in search of richer grasslands, fresh water, or to escape harsh weather, the early peoples of the Americas also moved. This pattern of following migrating animals would remain for prehistoric peoples around the world from the Americas to Africa to Asia.

Although hunters in North America stalked woolly mammoths, they did not use bows and arrows, as in this drawing. Instead, ancient hunters mostly used spears. Bows and arrows did not come into use in the Western Hemisphere until about A.D. 550.

Anthropologists identify two main stone ages, the Paleolithic and Neolithic ages. The Paleolithic Age, lasted much longer than the Neolithic. It stretched back in time to span, not just thousands of years, but 2 million. *Paleolithic* is a term used by anthropologists. It comes from two Greek words: *paleo*, meaning "old," and *lithic* meaning "stone." In other words, Paleolithic means "Old Stone Age." In time, the Paleolithic Age gave way to the Neolithic Age, or "New Stone Age," beginning around 10,000 B.C.[10]

Living in a New World

While the date for the earliest human inhabitants of the Americas remains a mystery, it is clear that people were in America about fifteen thousand years ago, toward the end of the most recent ice age. By that date, the fossil record of early humans becomes clearer. Archaeologists have found evidence of humans living at that time in eastern Siberia and in places scattered across western Alaska. It is assumed that humans also lived in Beringia, but with the end of the ice age, Beringia was covered by the ocean waters as the northern glaciers shrank. Documenting the humans of Beringia is nearly impossible, since that land has been underwater for the past ten thousand years. (Anthropologists have discovered mammoth fossils on the seabed where Beringia was once exposed.)

Once the first humans arrived in America, they began to scatter about, filling in the landscape. The process of migrating to the far reaches of the Western Hemisphere did not take place overnight. Scientists estimate that several thousand years passed before humans reached the farthest southern point in South America, Tierra del Fuego. Evidence exists that humans settled there around 7000 B.C.[11] People arrived in other parts of the Americas even earlier. By 12,000 B.C., humans had arrived in the eastern portion of the United States.[12] At the Meadowcroft site in Pennsylvania, which has been under excavation for years, archaeologists claim to have uncovered human artifacts dating to 15,000 B.C.[13] To the south, in modern-day Virginia, the Thunderbird site, located in the Shenandoah Valley, human relics dating to 10,000 B.C. have been unearthed.[14]

So, once people reached the Americas, how were they able to survive? How did they find food? As the earliest Americans spread throughout the continents, they began to find ways to survive and soon developed their own unique cultures.

Chapter 3

Finding Ways to Survive

Regardless of when the earliest humans arrived in the Western Hemisphere, the door of opportunity did not remain open forever. A warming trend brought about a receding of the polar ice cap and a gradual altering of the North American climate. Over the next several thousand years, until approximately 8000 B.C., the Pleistocene Era came to an end. Most of the animals that disappeared during this period were large ones, ranging from approximately one hundred pounds in weight to the four-ton woolly mammoths. These included the ancient horse and camel,[1] as well as a saber-toothed cat called *Smilodon*.[2]

North America was transformed as the glaciers retreated. Each part of the continent witnessed new patterns of temperature, seasons, rainfall, and wind. But through all this great change in animal and plant life, one ancient animal did not die out. The Pleistocene Era left behind the bison. These shaggy beasts were relatively quick, thus able to outrun humans. With other previously hunted animals no longer available, early American Indians began to hunt bison and learned to adapt their hunting methods and tools to this fast-moving target. Living in a continuing age of stone, the peoples of North America made changes in how they shaped their tools and weapons.

Paleolithic Hunting

For thousands of years, ancient hunters in the Americas primarily used spears and javelins in stalking their animal prey. A spear is a simple weapon consisting of a long wooden shaft, mounted at one end with a stone tip, which anthropologists and archaeologists call a projectile point. (Most nonexperts simply refer to such points as spear points today.) These points were fashioned out of stone and used for a variety of tools and weapons. Such points serve as one of the earliest examples of a hand-fashioned tool.

Stone was always a durable material to use in making tools and weapons. Not all types of stone could be easily reshaped into something by early peoples, so they relied on certain types of stone. They realized early the value of a rock with a sharpened edge. Over long spans of time, they refined their skills in making stone tools, producing such useful items as drills, awls, choppers, and blades of volcanic glass chipped to a razor's edge.

This Clovis spear point is significant because it was found at a bison kill site near Woodward, Oklahoma, where the nomadic people typically hunted mammoths.

A new stone technology came into use around 10,000 B.C. This new style of working stone produced a highly stylized, extremely functional weapon. It was unique in shape, having both balance and grace. It was a projectile form known today as a Clovis point. This special point type was found in 1932 in the ribs of a long-dead woolly mammoth near the town of Clovis, New Mexico, after which the point was named. It would not be until the 1950s that this point was dated using radio-carbon testing, which was not available as a technology until then. The point was eleven thousand five hundred years old.[3]

First Migration of Immigrants

Different groups of Asians migrated to the Americas. Anthropologists believe that those who migrated to the Western Hemisphere from Asia and Siberia came in a series of migrations. Those who arrived during the first migration entered the Americas across Beringia prior to 12,000 B.C. The majority of these migrants remained in northern and western Canada. Another movement of immigrants to the Western Hemisphere arrived later. They came by boat around 5000 B.C., long after Beringia was already underwater. Until 2000 B.C. these latecomers, known today as the Inuit, settled all across western Alaska, including the Aleutian Island chain. They extended their settlements across the frozen north

of Canada, settling on both the east and west shores of Hudson Bay. In time, these people settled as far east as Greenland. In fact, it would be the Inuit who would make contact with the Norsemen called Vikings around A.D. 1000. The Vikings, (European Scandinavians) would represent the next significant phase of migration to America.[4]

Early American Agriculture

Beyond hunting and gathering, early American Indians tapped other sources for food. They fished the streams, rivers, lakes, and coastal waters, which were abundant with fish, shellfish, and other marine life. These sources—hunting, gathering, fishing—all served ancient peoples in the Americas well, depending on where they lived.

But, in time, early Americans developed a completely different method of getting food for themselves. This method proved to be one they could rely on more readily than hunting or fishing. This was the practice of farming, or systematic agriculture. In the Western Hemisphere, this shift from hunting and gathering first occurred in Mexico.[5] Here, American Indians grew not only maize, a type of corn, but also a wide variety of other crops. These included beans, squash, gourds, tomatoes, peppers, and avocados. Central America, including Mexico, was also the source for cacao (which is used to make chocolate) and vanilla beans. Today, crops such as potatoes and corn are staple foods for hundreds of millions of people in the Americas.

American Indian Cultural Regions

By the time of the arrival of Europeans to America in the 1500s, the Western Hemisphere was home to millions of people. Scientists estimate that 12 million people lived in North, South, and Central America. If that number is correct, it means that one out of every seven people living in the world at that time called the Western Hemisphere his or her home. Such a population would have been equal to the population of Europe at that time. Of the 12 million inhabitants, about 15 to 20 percent, perhaps 2 million people, lived in North America, including the United States and Canada.[6]

These first residents of the Americas began to develop their own unique culture regions about five hundred years before the arrival of Columbus in 1492. Across what is today the United States, extending north into Canada, four distinct culture regions can be identified. By the year 1500, the people of the cultural groups found in each region had developed into distinct nations. The first modern nations, then, were largely in place by the time Europeans began to arrive. While anthropologists often describe them differently, American Indians

Chapter 4

People of the Southwest

The Southwest Desert culture region is a vast land of deserts that stretches across the modern-day states of Arizona and New Mexico, spreading north into the southern half of Utah, the southwestern third of Colorado, a slice of western Texas, southeastern Nevada, and southern California. The landscape of the region is rugged. Painted deserts, snowcapped mountains, and rocky canyons of yellow, brown, and red sandstone abound. It is the region of great saguaro cacti. Landforms found in the region include the Grand Canyon and the monoliths of eroded rock of Arizona's Monument Valley.[1] This is a land where annual rainfall is only a few inches.

Early Southwestern Peoples

Prior to the development of the later American Indians of the American Southwest, people worked hard to tame the region as they developed unique cultures to fit the land

and its climate. As the people of the ancient Southwest developed, they produced three types of cultures. They are known today as the Mogollons, the Hohokam, and the Anasazi. Each made a unique contribution to the culture of the Southwest region.

The Mogollon (muggy-OWN) were located in the southern half of the present-day state of New Mexico and southeastern Arizona. Mogollon people could also be found in the northern Mexican provinces of Chihuahua and Sonora.

The Mogollon were the first Southwestern people to adopt a culture that included agriculture, the building of permanent housing, and the making of pottery. Their farming included the "Three Sisters" (corn, beans, and squash), as well as cotton for clothing and tobacco for ceremonial purposes. Like the prehistoric people who settled the Southwest before them, the Mogollon built permanent encampments.[2] By A.D. 1100, the Mogollon began constructing adobe structures above ground. Such buildings resembled, to later Spanish explorers, apartment buildings in Spain. Thus, they named the homes of the Mogollon *pueblos*. (The word pueblo in Spanish means town or village.)

Since these ancient people grew cotton, they eventually developed into skilled weavers, creating elaborate blankets and clothing complete with feathers and animal furs for decoration. Their pottery was originally a simple

41

style, involving laying coils or ropes of brown clay on top of one another and then smoothing them out and firing them to dry and harden. One group of Mogollon people, the Mimbres, developed a highly stylized type of painted pottery that featured black paint on a white background.[3]

At the same time the Mogollons were flourishing, the Southwest witnessed the rise of another culture group—this one to the west—called the Hohokam. The name comes from the Pima nation of later centuries, who referred to these early people as "hohokam"—"the ancient ones." The Hohokam lived in south-central Arizona, in the valleys of the San Pedro, Salt, and Gila rivers. They farmed, built adobe houses, and made pottery. Their agriculture was so extensive that it provided nearly their entire diet. Their cornfields thrived because the Hohokam were very skilled at irrigation. They built water canals and ditches to divert water runoff to their fields.[4]

The center of Hohokam culture was located in a community called Snaketown, where the Hohokam lived for fifteen hundred years. The site lies south of present-day Phoenix.[5]

Ancient Cliff Dwellers

The third cultural group to develop in the region of the ancient Southwest was the Anasazi. The name means

This art by the ancient Anasazi is in Mesa Verde, Colorado. Scientists called these ancient artworks petroglyphs.

"ancient enemies" in the Navajo language. Anasazi culture began taking shape around 100 B.C. and was centered on the "four corners" plateau, where four states—Colorado, Utah, Arizona, and New Mexico— meet.[6] The Anasazi culture developed through a series of stages. In the earliest stage (100 B.C.–A.D. 400), the Anasazi lived in pit houses. They were hunter-gatherers, yet they also practiced a basic agriculture. They hunted with spears and snares, and used the *atlatl*, a device used to help give their darts and spears greater accuracy and power.[7]

During the second phase of Anasazi culture (c. A.D. 400–700), these people lived in pit homes lined with flat stones, covered with wooden timbers and brush. By this era, they had use of the bow and arrow. (Bows were in use among American Indians in modern-day Canada as early as A.D. 200. They reached the Great Plains around A.D. 550).[8] They had also domesticated the turkey, and their crops included the "Three Sisters" of corn, beans, and squash. In the decorative arts, these people produced turquoise bracelets, shell jewelry, and clay effigies, or symbolic figures of humans.[9]

By the third stage of development (A.D. 700–1100), the Anasazi were building elaborate pueblo systems that were multistoried, with dozens of rooms connected together, providing small apartments for living space.[10] The upper stories were reached by using ladders.

Eventually, the Anasazi began building new spiritual centers called *kivas*. These were often more elaborate than their homes. One of the most elaborate of the pueblos built during this period is found in the desert of northwestern New Mexico, a site called Pueblo Bonito, which is, according to historian Alvin M. Josephy, "the architectural jewel of the canyon."[11]

Today, Pueblo Bonito offers breathtaking views of the ruins of the Anasazi.

45

Pueblo Bonito

Centered in Chaco Canyon, Pueblo Bonito was an intricate complex of eight hundred rooms built in the shape of a half circle. The pueblo rose from the desert floor to a height of five stories. Other structures at Pueblo Bonito include large kivas used for ceremonial purposes. This site may have been home to as many as one thousand people.

Chaco Canyon provided these ancient Southwest inhabitants with an ideal setting for desert living.

An Economy Etched in Stone

Among the most important goods traded at Pueblo Bonito was a single type of stone that served as the backbone of the desert economy—turquoise. The stone could be mined in New Mexico. To traders from the extensive and advanced civilizations to the south, in Mexico, turquoise was "more valuable . . . than gold or jade."[12] Once the raw mineral was excavated out of regional mines by Anasazi miners and craftsmen, the turquoise was cut into small tiles.

Then, through Mesoamerican merchants and traders, the beautiful desert stones were delivered south. There, they would be cut into a variety of shapes and polished for jewelry and other decorative items. For more than a century, the turquoise trade fueled the economy of Pueblo Bonito. In exchange for goods from California and Mexico, the Anasazi delivered the precious turquoise to those willing to pay premium prices.

Although the region had little vegetation and few trees, the Anasazi of Chaco, according to Josephy, created a "center for their civilization—a place where traders exchanged goods and spiritual pilgrimages ended."[13]

Pueblo Bonito and its outlying communities established a thriving urban complex in the Southwest deserts of today's northern New Mexico. Its one thousand residents utilized six hundred rooms for their homes, shops, and merchant centers; government houses; and social gathering places. A grand plaza sat in the center of the D-shaped village with five-story buildings standing above the common meeting grounds.

But, at the heart of life at Pueblo Bonito was the kiva system. These underground temples can still be found throughout the canyon, but the main complex is located at Pueblo Bonito. Here the Anasazi delivered many wooden timbers to provide the roof supports for these religious centers. These social and religious centers provided the compass for the settlement, giving them religious direction even as the mysteries of the kiva remained secret from nearly everyone but those who entered into these sunken chambers.

The building process found at Pueblo Bonito continued into the next Anasazi phase (c. A.D. 1100–1300). By this time, the Anasazi had developed into occupation groups that included weavers, farmers, potters, and other craftsmen. Weavers produced cotton fabrics that

were dyed in bright colors and decorated with feathers. During this period, sites such as Pueblo Bonito were abandoned, as the Anasazi's desert culture began to unravel. While Chaco Canyon had built a grand civilization that was both sophisticated and creative, the days of the Anasazi in the canyon were always numbered.[14]

What caused the decline at Pueblo Bonito remains unclear. Archaeologists do know that other groups of people in the Southwest, including those in Arizona and Nevada, also began to trade in turquoise as rivals to Chaco. Perhaps so much turquoise became available that the value of the once precious stone began to decline. In addition, one of Chaco's most important and longtime markets for turquoise, the Toltec capital in Mexico, Tula, fell into civil conflict, thus cutting off this formerly reliable trade partner.

While all these circumstances may have led to the collapse of life at Pueblo Bonito, a natural calamity might have been the greater villain. Beginning around A.D. 1130, a fifty-year-long drought cycle set in throughout the region of Chaco Canyon. This drought probably dried up nearly all local water sources. The result was that by the end of the twelfth century, Chaco Canyon was abandoned—its buildings left to crumble, its turquoise markets having dried up, as connections with Mesoamerica blew away like a hot desert wind.

With the collapse of important sites such as Chaco Canyon, the Anasazi did not die out, but simply moved on. Other sites came into use, such as Mesa Verde, located in southwestern Colorado, and Canyon de Chelly in northeastern Arizona. From the Spanish words for "green table," Mesa Verde was built into the rock cliffs of the Colorado Plateau. The cliff-side village reached its height around A.D. 1200.

Cliff dwellings can still be seen at Mesa Verde in Colorado.

While Pueblo Bonito had been built on an exposed site on the floor of Chaco Canyon, the Mesa Verde Indians, many of whom probably came from Chaco or were the descendents of those who had formerly lived there, built their homes into the sides of the canyon under great rockshelters and overhangs. At its height, Mesa Verde was home to thousands of residents, living in houses similar to those built at Chaco, sheltered by the rocks. Among the largest of these cliff dwellings was one referred to by archaeologists as the Cliff Palace. (Despite its significance today as a major tourist attraction in the southwest corner of Colorado, Mesa Verde was not occupied by nearly the number of Anasazi who lived in nearby Montezuma Valley. Perhaps thirty thousand called that valley their home.) While the canyon overhangs sheltered the villages at Mesa Verde, the lands above the canyon walls were the real centers of economic activity. Here, Anasazi villagers worked the local fields, "reaching their town by climbing the sheer cliff walls with finger and toe-holds."[15]

By the end of the thirteenth century, the Anasazi of the cliff dwellings began to abandon their homes—the environment ultimately proving too hostile. Examination of tree rings reveals the years 1276–1299 as part of a drought cycle in the region. The threat of hostile neighboring peoples, such as the Athabascan (the Navajo and the Apache), also drove the Anasazi from their homes. The final era of the Anasazi (1300–1550) was one of transition, as they developed into the American Indians known as the Pueblo. During this period, tens of thousands of Anasazi abandoned their cliff dwellings and established themselves to the east, along the banks of the Rio Grande Valley. Here, they built new towns, near the security of water—Alcanfor, Taos, Piro, and others that they were still occupying when the Spanish arrived in the region by the 1500s. Still others found new lives to the west in Hopi and Zuni towns in modern-day Arizona. As the decades passed, the Navajo arrived in the region and took over control of the lands that had formerly been dominated by the Anasazi.

Pueblo Peoples

When the Spanish explorers arrived in the American Southwest in the 1540s, the written record of the Indians of the Southwest began. The Spanish named these American Indians the "Pueblo," after the Spanish word for village. The name is still used today by the Pueblo people. The term is a general one that refers to the nations known as the Hopi and Zuni of the Colorado Plateau region. Additional Southwestern nations are the Hualapai, Havasupai, and Yavapai groups, desert farmers of central and northern Arizona, as well as the Pima

51

These Pueblo ruins are located at Wupatki National Monument.

and Papago, the Navajo and the Chiricahua, and the Mimbreno and Mescalero Apache.

Life among the Pueblo was generally peaceful, secure, and creative. Both men and women were skilled in handicrafts, producing a variety of goods including baskets, pottery, and textiles. Pueblo women made pottery and baskets. Basket styles varied from tribe to tribe. Their baskets were often woven into shallow containers and colored with vegetable dyes of yellow, purple, green, blue, and black, often decorated with geometric patterns. Some pottery was made to use in the home, but other pieces were produced for ceremonial use or for their beauty. Local clay deposits were used, and the pots were made by coiling, smoothing out the coils, then firing them.

The women also did the cooking. The Southwestern nations were farmers who relied heavily on maize as their chief food crop. They grew other crops, as well, including kidney beans, squash, gourds, sunflowers, and Aztec beans. The Spanish introduced the Southwestern inhabitants to wheat, onions, peaches, watermelons, and the ever-popular chili pepper. As for the men, they provided food through hunting. They stalked deer, antelope, rabbits, and even coyotes. Although the bow and arrow were used, the Pueblo also used clubs and boomerangs.

Village and Religious Life

The Pueblo peoples were not historically led by warrior bands and societies as other regional culture groups were, but instead relied on various religious societies. Each society had a kiva in the village and had responsibility for a specific task, such as hunting, military defense, political leadership, or medicinal cures for tribal diseases. Each society was led by its own priests, who could hand down decisions affecting the entire group.

Perhaps the most important religious society of the Pueblo was the *kachina* group. All its members were

male and they were split into six divisions, representing
north, south, east, west, up, and down. Each division had
its own kiva in which to carry out ceremonies and secret
rituals. Kachina priests were responsible for everything
related to the masked dances. In most tribes, each kachina kiva group sponsored three dances annually. These
kachina priests were thought to be representations or
symbols of either the Pueblo's gods or the spirits of the
dead. They wore masks and elaborate costumes for use
during tribal ceremonies. Kachina masks were thought
to be so powerful that each one was burned after the
death of its wearer.[16]

In the East

While Southwestern cultures were developing, several
American Indian nations in the East were also building
societies. Some of these eastern nations would build tow-
ering mounds of earth and another would form an early
democracy, or government of the people.

Chapter 5

The Mound Builders and the Iroquois

Early inhabitants of the lands west of the Mississippi developed into the Eastern culture group. This group is often divided into the subregions of the Northeast and Southeast. The early inhabitants of the Northeast lived in a temperate climate with distinct seasons. The summers were hot and the winters could be bitterly cold. Yet these early people adapted to fit their environment. The Northeast region stretched from Canada's easternmost provinces to the coast of New England and south to the Chesapeake Bay. Settlement in the region ran to the west where the Great Lakes provided an extensive water system for these peoples and their canoes.

The land was originally covered with thick forests of oak, chestnut, maple, and hickory trees. The early hunter-gatherers used Clovis spear points to hunt the abundant wildlife. Around 7000 B.C., the region developed a warmer climate, and a new culture developed: the Archaic. The

people of this region became more dependent on deer, nuts, and wild grains for their food. Around 3000 B.C., the American Indians of the Northeast achieved a new level of culture. They planted seeds, grew squash, and, out toward the Great Lakes, they farmed sunflowers and marsh elder. Sunflower seeds were ground into flour for bread. The people of this era expanded their fishing and shellfish gathering activities, including catching swordfish off the coast of Maine. In the area of the Great Lakes, these people who had relied on stone tools began to work with copper, which was abundant. They fashioned it into tools, blades, spearheads, and ornaments.[1]

During this Early Woodland Stage, which lasted from 1000 to 100 B.C., the Indians of the East were noted for the building of earthen mounds. The most important mound-building culture was the Adena culture, which eventually developed a highly structured social order. The Adena culture was named for an archaeological site located on the Ohio River in the modern-day state of Ohio. They built permanent villages and burial mounds.[2]

A new culture developed, which was called the Middle Woodland. Beginning about 100 B.C. and lasting until about A.D. 500, the period witnessed another phase of mound building, called the Hopewellian Era. During this era, the peoples of the Northeast began planting and harvesting new crops, including tobacco and some maize. They were busy making stone, wood, and metal tools and weapons and constructed large burial sites, burying their dead with their belongings.

The people of this era lived in wigwams—oval structures with curved, dome-like roofs. These houses were covered with bark or animal skins. Inside such houses, the American Indians kept a variety of household items. Hopewellian women fashioned elaborately decorated clay pots to use for cooking and food storage. The men carved stone tobacco pipes in the shapes of animals and human heads, and musical instruments including reed pipes and flutes, drums, and animal rattles.[3]

In the Northeast, from 1000 to the 1400s, just prior to the arrival of Europeans, the people of the region began to develop into modern nations. These nations include the Delaware, Micmac, Illinois, Shawnee, Narragansett, and the Haudenosaunee, otherwise known by their enemies as the Iroquois.[4]

The Mississippi Mound Builders

The Southeastern culture region of the United States was the homeland of a wide variety of Indian nations prior to the coming of Europeans to the New World. This vast region extends west from the Atlantic Ocean to the Mississippi River, and from the Gulf of Mexico north to the Ohio River. These lands provided a home to dozens of American Indian groups for thousands of years.

While little is known about the origins of the people of the Southeast, archaeologists do know they were producing pottery in the region as early as 2000 B.C. Around A.D. 700, a dominant culture rose in the region, which modern archaeologists refer to as the Mississippian culture or the Middle Mississippian. This culture was centered along several key southeastern river systems, including the Illinois, Tennessee, the lower Ohio, and the middle Mississippi rivers. It is thought to be part of a series of mound-building peoples of the ancient world, preceded by the Adena, Poverty Point, and the Hopewell cultures.[5]

This era of Mound Builders lasted from A.D. 700 until the time of the arrival of Europeans along the Mississippi River in the 1500s. When compared to the Adena and Hopewell cultures, the striking difference about the mounds built in the Mississippian period is that these American Indians built mounds of earthen pyramids. While earlier mounds were apparently constructed as burial sites, the Mississippian pyramids served as temple bases and, occasionally, as the base for a powerful ruler's house.

During the Mississippian phase, a new variety of corn was introduced to the region from Mexico. The Indians of the Southeast continued to farm the land. The Mississippians developed major towns and a true city. It was the great Southeastern city of Cahokia, located in the region where the Mississippi and Missouri rivers join one another. Cahokia was situated on the eastern bank of the Mississippi River opposite present-day St. Louis, Missouri. Cahokia was home to about twenty-five thousand to thirty thousand people, while an additional twenty-five thousand lived in villages that surrounded the ancient city.[6]

The Etawah Indian mounds are located outside the town of Cartersville, Georgia.

Mounds of History

Archaeologists have unearthed at least eighty-five mounds at Cahokia. Some were as high as ten-story buildings. The mounds were built by workers who carried basket loads of earth to these sites. The largest—today known as Monk's Mound—was erected in fourteen stages, from A.D. 900 to 1150. The mound covers sixteen acres and stands one hundred feet high. Mississippian culture reached its height of significance somewhere between the eleventh and twelfth centuries A.D. By the early 1600s, the ancient Mississippian centers had been abandoned—the population perhaps killed off by starvation, drought, or destruction by an enemy.[7]

The Last of the Mound Builders: The Natchez

Although Cahokia had been abandoned by the arrival of the Europeans in the 1500s, later Mississippian cultures did survive until then, including the Natchez. When the Spanish explorer Hernando de Soto arrived on the banks of the Mississippi River in 1540, the Natchez numbered about four thousand people living in at least nine town settlements scattered along the Mississippi River.

These last of the mound-building cultures remained

relatively intact well into the 1600s. The Natchez were ruled by a powerful king called the Great Sun, who lived in the largest of the Natchez settlements, the Great Village, located near modern-day Natchez, Mississippi. The belief within the nation was that the Great Sun had descended from the sun, which was considered all-powerful. As a result, the people worshipped the Great Sun, just as groups in Mexico (Aztec) and South America (Inca) honored their exalted rulers.[8]

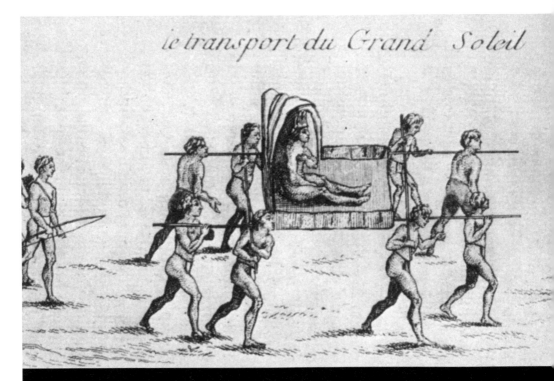

le transport du Grand Soleil

"The Great Sun," the ruler of the Natchez, is carried to a harvest festival. This sketch was done by Antoine Le Page du Pratz for his 1758 account of the Natchez.

Daily life among the Natchez centered around agriculture. They produced crops, and the most important among them was maize. In addition, they harvested edible seeds and plants. When the Natchez first made contact with Europeans, they were introduced to a variety of new foods that became so important to them that they named some of their lunar months after them. The thirteen lunar months of the Natchez were Deer, Strawberries, Little Corn, Watermelons, Peaches, Mulberries, Great Corn, Turkeys, Bison, Bears, Cold Meal, Chestnuts, and Nuts. At least two of the foods—watermelons and peaches—were brought to America by Europeans.

Natchez houses were rectangular with bent tree saplings used to provide a curving roof. The roofs were covered with thatch grasses. The sides were covered with adobe mud and whitewashed. They were dark inside, because light entered only through the door.

By the 1700s, Natchez relations with French traders had deteriorated into war. In 1729, the Natchez revolted against the French who were preparing to destroy the Great Village to make way for a French governor's plantation. The Natchez and the French went to war, leaving many on both sides dead. But the Natchez were ultimately defeated. Surviving Natchez were scattered among neighboring American Indian nations. However, the descendants of the Natchez and the cultures associated with the Mound Builders live on. Among those descendants are the Cherokee, Chickasaw, Choctaw, Seminole, and Creek.

The Haudenosaunee

Even though the mound-building phase of the Eastern Indians faded away, other culture groups continued on, developing into modern American Indian nations. The Northeast became home to many different Indian groups scattered along the coasts, lake country, and river valleys. While the system of nations was distinctly in place by the time of the arrival of the European explorers after A.D. 1500, there were many different cultural groups, some of whom were bitter enemies.

The Haudenosaunee, the people also known as the Iroquois, lived in present-day Ontario, Canada, and in upstate New York. This group has lived in this region for over one thousand years. They were among the first of the Northeastern nations to adopt intensive agriculture, shifting away from a reliance on native plants, fishing, and hunting. The Haudenosaunee raised corn, beans, squash, and sunflowers.

Haudenosaunee, meaning "People of the Long House," was an alliance of five Iroquois groups. The Haudenosaunee constructed wooden, bark-covered homes that were, indeed, quite long. On average, the Haudenosaunee longhouses were fifty to one hundred

feet long and about twenty-five feet wide.[9] The roof was barrel shaped, supported by a line of ridge poles running the length of the house. The peak of the house was about twenty feet high. Some longhouses were much larger, measuring about three hundred feet in length![10]

Other Northeastern people lived in different styles of housing. The Algonquian built wigwams, which housed fewer people and thus fewer families together. They were much smaller than the longhouses, and were

A typical Iroquois village had a number of longhouses inside a palisade, or protective wall.

designed as bark-covered domes with a center rising to a height slightly taller than an adult male. The wigwam might measure fourteen by twenty feet. Another difference between the longhouse and the wigwam lay in who built each. Iroquois men built the longhouses, while Algonquian women built their wigwams. Several families usually shared the inside of an Iroquois longhouse. There were multiple fire sites; two families, occupying opposite sides of the house, shared each site.[11]

The Iroquois lived in a matrilineal society. This meant that women provided the basis for the family, and children were born into their mother's clan, her extended family. Iroquois women also served as clan leaders. The Iroquois also formed another unique social and political structure among themselves. During the 1500s, before the first Europeans reached their lands, the Haudenosaunee formed a confederacy of five nations— the Onondaga, Seneca, Oneida, Mohawk, and Cayuga. (A sixth nation, the Tuscarora, joined in 1713.) This confederacy was a type of democratic league in which every nation had an equal voice. The League of the Six Nations would serve as an example of New World cooperation among American Indians.[12]

All Northeastern tribes had a variety of diets, supplied through farming, gathering, fishing, and hunting. Farming among the Haudenosaunee was done by the women while the men hunted, caught fish, and traded

The Symbolic Longhouse

The Iroquois Confederacy was also sometimes known as the
Great League of Peace and Power. The confederacy gave
the Haudenosaunee their identity. The longhouse was a symbol
of their cooperation. Every nation of the confederacy had its
special, symbolic place. The Seneca served as the keepers of
the western door, while the Mohawk were the keepers of the
east entrance. (Iroquois longhouses were situated east to west.)
The Onondaga maintained the symbolic fire in the center
of the symbolic longhouse. Inside the house, between the
Onondaga and the Seneca, to the west were the Cayuga.
The Oneida were situated in the east wing of the longhouse,
between the Onondaga and the Mohawk.[13]

with distant nations. Farming was not easy for these
people since the growing season of the Northeast is
short. Hunting was easy in the Northeast, since game
was plentiful. The Algonquians hunted deer, caribou,
moose, elk, and bear. They also hunted smaller animals,
including raccoons, muskrats, porcupines, woodchucks,
and beaver, as well as ducks, geese, and grouse.

The Haudenosaunee raised the "Three Sisters" in
great variety. They produced sixty types of beans, eight

varieties of squash, and many different kinds of corn, including popcorn, which they mixed with maple syrup.

Eastern Woodlands Religion and Mythology

Both the Iroquois and the Algonquians recognized a spirit, or god, that was present in the entire natural world around them. Though similar in nature, each nation gave their all-knowing spirit a different name. The Iroquois called their great spirit Orenda; the Algonquian referred to theirs as Manitou. These supernatural beings were actually the embodiment of many spirits, which lived and occupied all the objects common to each American Indian's existence.

Most Eastern nations recognized a special class of religious leaders called *shamans*, who were thought to have great power, including healing the sick. While shamans wielded great spiritual power as holy men, other men filled additional roles as prophets, magicians, and as great healers who used herbs. Algonquian magicians or sorcerers claimed power over some aspects of the physical world including the ability to halt the coming of natural disasters. The Algonquian believed in magic because there were many things for which they had no explanation.

Squash and beans were an important part of the
diet of many American Indians, including the
Iroquois. Indians hollowed out and dried squash
to make bowls and musical instruments, like this
Iroquois rattle (inset).

False Face Societies

Healers could be found among the Iroquois as well. Some of their medicine men formed a special group called the False Face Society, whose purpose was not only to heal the diseased, but also to keep them from getting sick in the first place. To do this, they carved wooden masks that bore hideous and contorted facial features designed to protect the tribe by scaring off evil spirits that carried disease. While each mask was handmade and no two were ever exactly alike, there were about a dozen basic false-face designs. Some featured askew mouth formations, others had protruding tongues, and still others with thick lips and mocking looks.[14]

Beyond the East

In addition to the Eastern American Indian cultures, there were also many Indian nations in a region called the Great Plains. This area spreads across the central portion of the United States. There, American Indians forged many vibrant cultures.

The American Indians of the Great Plains region often hunted bison, also called buffalo.

Chapter 6

Hunting on the Great Plains

For many people, their mental picture of American Indians includes people wearing war paint, riding horses, living in cone-shaped tepees, hunting buffalo, smoking peace pipes, and wearing great feathered headdresses. However, these images create a limited view of the rich differences found between traditional American Indian groups. The Indians who embody these images were those who made the Great Plains their home.

The region of the Great Plains is gigantic. It sweeps across the borders of two nations today, the United States and Canada. Extending from the area of the Mississippi River to the foothills of the Rocky Mountains, the Great Plains were vast, often empty grasslands, today broken up by thousands of farms and ten thousand cities, towns, and villages. From north to south, the Great Plains include three Canadian provinces—Alberta, Manitoba, and Saskatchewan—as well as all or part of over a dozen states.[1]

The history of the American Indians of the Plains predates the arrival of Europeans (who introduced the horse to the Western Hemisphere) by as many as eleven thousand years. At first these American Indians moved from place to place, following animals they hunted. During later centuries, eastern Plains peoples lived in relatively permanent villages and practiced agriculture. Nevertheless, hunting still provided an additional source of food.[2]

Early Plains Life

The earliest residents of the Great Plains region were nomadic hunters who lived on the land between eleven thousand and seven thousand years ago. These peoples hunted the great woolly mammoths and ancient bison. Between 5000 and 2500 B.C., the Plains peoples nearly abandoned the region completely, driven both east and west by a warming trend that rendered the Plains inhospitable. The great animals of the Pleistocene Era left the region, some becoming extinct, leaving those humans left on the Plains with only smaller animals to hunt, such as the pronghorn antelope.[3]

Around 2500 B.C., people began to return to the Great Plains in increasing numbers. Many came to the Plains from the lands they occupied in the Eastern Woodlands. A new culture developed during the Plains Woodland period, which was firmly in place

A rock engraving at the Plains Indian Museum in Cody, Wyoming, depicts a warrior with a feathered headdress. The engraving is between twenty-five hundred and thirty-five hundred years old.

between the years 500 B.C. and A.D. 1000. In the midst of that period, sometime between A.D. 200 and 400, the people of the Plains had developed a stable, semi-permanent village life in what is today eastern Kansas, Nebraska, Colorado, northeastern Oklahoma, and along the course of the Missouri River from present-day Missouri to the Dakotas.

These American Indians planted corn and beans for food, while still depending on hunting and gathering wild plants. The use of pottery was in place during these centuries, and Indians fashioned tools and weapons from stone and bone. A few artifacts were hammered out of copper.[4]

By A.D. 900, a new migration of American Indians from the Eastern Woodlands found their way out onto the Plains, bringing new settlements and villages to the vast expanses of the eastern Plains. Just as the old villages had been, these new Indian settlements were built along the major rivers of the region. These new arrivals introduced new crops to the region, such as squash and sunflowers. They constructed square or rectangular earthen lodges, which were surrounded by a wooden fence or palisade, as was the custom of many nations of the Eastern Woodlands. These Plains Indians hunted bison, driving them over cliffs. This method of hunting bison required an Indian runner to lure the bison into following him until he led them to a precipice where the animals fell to their deaths. The runner might jump a short distance to a narrow shelf for safety. While the men hunted, the women practiced farming, using digging sticks to plant seeds and hoeing their fields using hoes fashioned from bison scapula, the animal's shoulder blade.[5]

By 1500, a drought on the Plains caused American Indians to abandon many of their settlements in the western half of the region. About this same time, Plains cultural groups began to make greater contact with one another, although they might be separated by hundreds of miles of treeless prairie. New American Indian cultures developed larger villages and a greater reliance on agriculture. Villages also became more permanent. Earthen lodges became larger and were now circular rather than rectangular.[6]

The nations that were established on the Great Plains by the time Europeans began reaching their lands, beginning with the Spanish in the early 1500s, were varied. Situated along the lower Missouri River basin, were the Iowa, Kansas, Missouri, Omaha, Osage, Otoe, and Ponca. The middle course of the Missouri River was home to the Arikara, Hidatsa, and Mandan. To the west, across the modern-day state of Nebraska were the Pawnee and to their south, the Wichita.[7]

Earthen Lodges of the Mandan

While most people picture the Plains Indians living in tepees, several nations with historical roots in this region did not. One such nation was the Mandan. These people migrated onto the Great Plains around 1100 from the Mississippi Valley and settled in the territory of what is today North Dakota, along the banks of the Missouri River. When the first whites arrived near the Mandan, the nation was living in the Big Bend region of the river. The American explorers Meriwether Lewis and William Clark stayed with the Mandan there during the winter of 1804–1805.

The Mandan lived in permanent settlements and practiced an extensive agriculture that included raising corn, beans, squash, sunflowers, and tobacco for ceremonial purposes. They made pottery for storage and cooking. They built their homes in the form of small earthen mounds rather than relying on the tepee design. Building a typical Mandan dwelling involved digging a pit measuring one to four feet in depth. This provided the floor for the lodge. A wooden frame was built up from the pit floor, and poles were lashed together, then covered with several layers of willow branches. On top of this wooden framework, the Mandan placed a layer of prairie grass to provide a roof covering and much needed insulation against the hot summers and frigid winters. Sod was then placed on top of the willow branches and grasses to provide the final roofing layer for the dwelling.[8]

These earthen houses had to provide warmth for the Mandan during the long winter months in a region where temperatures fell far below freezing. A Mandan

Mandan Indians perform the Bull Dance in this painting by George Catlin. Their earthen lodges are in the background.

Park officials built a replica of a Mandan earthen lodge at On-a-Slant Mandan Village on the Missouri River in North Dakota.

village ranged from ten to one hundred lodges. These rounded lodges with sunken floors served as home to several families who lived together, including as many as forty or fifty people, if not more. Each family provided its own beds, which were placed around the wall of the lodge circle. The lodges also provided shelter for the nation's dogs, and, in cases of severely cold temperatures, even their horses might be housed inside.

In the center of the dwelling a fire burned, providing additional warmth for the families living there, as well as heat for cooking. In the center of the roof, the Mandan left a hole for the fire's smoke to escape.[9] In all, eight Great Plains tribal groups lived for at least a majority of the year in such dwellings. In addition to the Mandan, these tribes included the Arikara, the Hidatsa, the Pawnee, the Omaha, the Caddo, the Wichita, and the Osage.

Military Societies

Warfare on the Great Plains was common between the nations living across this vast expanse of territory. Plains Indian fighting used a basic organization for warfare, the military society. Indian males belonged to such groups, typically entering them when they reached their early teen years. These societies imposed a specific code of behavior on their members, requiring them to learn

special songs and dances, and wear special insignia, indicating the military society to which they belonged.

While some societies were intertribal, allowing members from different nations, most were not. Some societies were extremely "closed," allowing only warriors who were invited to join the group. An invitation might be based on a warrior's personal record of exploits and deeds in battle. A nation typically boasted several military societies. The Kiowa had six such societies, including one for young boys, ages ten to twelve, who received early training to become warriors. Originally, the Cheyenne had five societies: the Fox, Elk (or Hoof Rattle), Shield, Bowstring, and the fiercest of all, the Dog Soldiers.

One of the greatest acts of courage a Plains warrior could carry out was the practice of "counting coup." While most cultures who engage in war expect to kill their enemy, the

Above, Atsina Indian chiefs are on horseback, with one holding a counting-coup stick. The Blackfoot Indians also used coup sticks (*inset*).

Plains Indians considered it more honorable to humiliate an enemy by merely touching him and perhaps allowing him to live. (The word *coup* is French, meaning "blow.") This practice was carried out with a coup stick, which a warrior carried into battle. The stick was not a real weapon, but was used to strike or hit an enemy. A warrior could "count coup" on an enemy using a true weapon, such as a bow, a lance, a club, or even just a hand. The purpose of the coup was to show its victim that an enemy was brave enough to come within range of being killed, sometimes armed with nothing but a stick, and that that warrior was able to touch his victim without himself being wounded or struck down.[10]

Plains Indians Religion

To the typical Indian of the Great Plains, the spirit world was a potent place, one which was interconnected with the natural world in which these American Indians found themselves. Plains Indians religion, as was true of all the American Indian nations, was by nature animistic. All things—plants, animals, the stars and planets, water, even rocks—had spirits whose qualities could, at least in part, be passed on to warriors who performed certain deeds. For many Great Plains Indians, a practice called the vision quest became an important avenue for making a connection between the natural world and the spirit world. Warriors sought "visions"

through an involved series of rituals. Usually, a male attempted his first vision quest as a teenager. The process often began with the building of a sweat lodge, something similar to a sauna, from tree saplings. The warrior sat inside and stones were heated. Water was poured over the hot rocks to create steam. The process of sitting in the hot steam "purified" the brave. He then stripped off his clothing, and painted his body with white clay. Then, he secluded himself outside the camp and fasted for several days.

After days of food and water deprivation, plus continuous exposure to the elements, the warrior hoped to receive a vision, actually an induced hallucination. Such visions were considered a window to the spirit world. If such a vision did not occur, the brave might then cut himself repeatedly, the resulting loss of blood often causing him to become semiconscious, and thus creating a trancelike state.[11]

Once the vision had taken place, the warrior then often related his dream to a medicine man who served as the vision's interpreter. Whatever was considered to be the vision's most potent symbol—an animal, a tree, a natural element—was then thought to be that warrior's guardian spirit. The brave then began collecting objects to serve as charms, which represented things he recalled from his vision. He placed the charms in a sacred pouch called a medicine bundle.

Medicine Bundles

These leather pouches were considered powerful medicine to the Plains Indians who carried them. They not only included objects remembered from visions, but also other items considered sacred by members of his tribe. Medicine bundles were thought to possess magical powers and brought good fortune to the warrior and his family. While individuals usually carried their own medicine bundles, many Plains Indian bands had medicine bundles of their own. Such bundles were held by tribal chiefs, medicine men, or shamans, and their contents were considered sacred to the entire band or even the nation. Sacred items, such as smoking pipes, often were found among the potent inventory of American Indians' medicine bundles.[12]

Sacred Pipes

Pipes were used in many of the sacred and ceremonial rituals of the Great Plains tribes. Such pipes were considered holy, sacred, and spiritually powerful. Individuals often made their own pipes, but many nations had pipes that belonged to the entire group. Most pipes were made of wood, sometimes with the stem extending several feet in length. Other pipes were fashioned out of a soft, reddish rock called catlinite. The most important catlinite quarry was located in

Minnesota. This quarry was itself considered sacred, and braves from many different nations came to the site. No warfare was to take place on this holy ground and enemies worked within sight of one another, carving out pieces of catlinite to fashion into pipe bowls and stems. Other Plains pipes were fashioned out of steatite, or soapstone. These pipes were typically decorated with porcupine quills, feathers, beads, and horsehair. Indians considered such pipes sacred, in part, because the tobacco burned in them was considered sacred.[13]

Out West

The American Indians of the West had different spiritual practices from those of the Great Plains. This is because the Indian groups of the West had their own rich histories that shaped them as a people.

Chapter 7

American Indians in the West

From the Rocky Mountains to the Pacific Coast, the American Indians of the West lived in several cultural subgroups—the Great Basin, Great Plateau, Pacific Northwest, and California. West of the Rocky Mountains and east of California's Sierra Nevada range lies an American Indian cultural region called the Great Basin. Vast mountains, including various lower ranges, surround the region. Since the area is at a lower elevation than its surroundings, it forms a natural "basin" for the region's rainfall.

Water has no natural outlet by which to flow out of the Great Basin, so it has historically collected in many lakes within the mountain-locked system. Since rivers and streams drain from the snowcapped mountains into these lakes, the lake water evaporates and then falls as rain once more. This cycle produces lakes of a higher than normal salt content, such as the Great Salt Lake of Utah.

Early Peoples of the Great Basin

Those American Indians living in the Great Basin always faced an environment that was hostile and arid. There were few types of plants. The region is dominated by juniper trees, sagebrush, and piñon trees, which have always been highly prized by the region's American Indians for their pine nuts. Large animal life in the region is typically sparse, forcing the occupants of the Great Basin to collect berries, roots, pine nuts, seeds, rodents, snakes, lizards, and grubs. Despite its arid and inhospitable surroundings, Indians have occupied the Great Basin for thousands of years. Archaeologists trace human occupation of the region back to perhaps eleven thousand five hundred years ago.[1]

About nine thousand years ago, the region was home to the desert culture, which relied on hunting. By that time, the large Pleistocene animals had died out. The American Indians of this period lived in caves, beneath rockshelters, and in wickiups, small huts fashioned from sticks, to protect themselves from the hot climate. Artifacts uncovered from this era include stone and wooden tools, such as digging sticks, wooden clubs, milling stones, and stone scrapping tools. Evidence of basket weaving, dating from around 7000 to 5000 B.C., has been unearthed in Danger Cave in western Utah.

Sometime before one thousand years ago, early Shoshonean-speaking arrivals entered the Great Basin and their descendants have remained there.[2]

Between 2000 B.C. and A.D. 1, the Basin population had developed into villages that were typically established near the region's lakes. Adapting further to the surrounding environment, these early villagers fished using hooks and nets. Hunting was still common. The Great Basin tribes practiced regular roundups of rabbits, antelopes, and even grasshoppers for eating. To aid in hunting ducks, they created duck decoys, woven out of grasses.

Agriculture was virtually nonexistent for these American Indians. They remained a gathering people, sending out regular parties of foragers into the greener lower valleys near their villages to collect seeds, berries, and nuts. Acorns and pine nuts were also gathered to be eaten.[3] They used digging sticks to dig up edible roots. White men who entered the region in more recent centuries called the American Indians in the Great Basin "Digger Indians." Despite all these efforts, food remained nearly a constant problem in the arid, bleak environment of the Great Basin.[4]

Today, the descendents of those who first occupied the lands of the Great Basin remain in the region. Among the most important nations of the Great Basin

"Digger Indians" return from a hunt carrying rabbits and
birds in the Sierra Nevada Mountains in the 1800s.

are the Western Shoshone, located in Nevada; the Paiute and Gosiute of Utah; the Washo and Mono of eastern California and western Nevada; and the Northern Shoshone (Wind River) of southwestern Wyoming.

Peoples of the Great Plateau

North of the Great Basin lies the region called the Great Plateau. The Plateau is between the Cascade Mountains of Oregon and Washington states and the Rocky Mountains. It extends north into Canada. Other smaller mountain chains give the Plateau an uneven landscape marked by peaks and valleys. The region is also drained by two vast river systems—the Fraser and the Columbia. The great northern bend of the Fraser system, located in the Canadian province of British Columbia, forms the northern boundary of the Plateau.[5]

Unlike the Great Basin, the Great Plateau is a region rich with life. It comprises portions of eastern Washington and Oregon, as well as the entire state of Idaho, a sliver of northern California, and much of Canadian British Columbia. The Great Plateau is thick with forests that have, for thousands of years, been home to all kinds of fur-bearing animals from grizzly bears to beavers, as well as horned animals, including deer, elk, antelope, and moose. The rivers, which wind through every corner of the region, teem with fish, including trout and sturgeon. But the prize fish of the

American Indians was salmon, the primary food source for the Indians of the Great Plateau for thousands of years.

This natural abundance has always been a magnet for about two dozen American Indian nations. In the southern part of the region were the Klamath, Modoc, Chinook, Salish, Nez Perce, Cayuse, and Palouse. To the north, the Flathead, Kalispel, Spokane, and Coeur d'Alene lived beyond the Columbia River. Because of their location in the interior portion of what is today the United States, the Great Plateau Indians did not make contact with Europeans until the 1700s. Even then, the contact was only occasional, consisting of bartering with French and British fur trappers and traders.[6]

Early California Natives

Long before the arrival of Europeans in the Western Hemisphere, great numbers of American Indians lived along the Pacific coastal lands as well as farther inland in a region known today as the state of California. From the coast to the Sierra Nevada mountain chain to the east, this temperate environment was a welcome place for hundreds of thousands of American Indians and scores of independent small nations. But the California culture region is a place of great extremes in topography and, to a lesser extent, climate. It included a northern region with greater rainfall and cooler temperatures

A Poma Indian woman cooks acorns in front of a type of home called a wickiup in California in 1924.

year-round. But to the south, the California Indians lived in a warmer environment, a region consisting of scrubby desert lands, similar to the Great Basin. Yet American Indians lived there in great numbers.

By the time of the arrival of Europeans to the New World, California peoples may have numbered as high as three hundred fifty thousand.[7] Nearly one hundred nations lived in the expansive region of California. In the north lived the Tolowa, Mattole, Hoopa, Wiyot, and Yurok. These nations sometimes borrowed culturally from the natives of the Pacific Northwest. In central California lived the Yuki, Karok, Shasta, and Yana. These nations were similar to those of the Plateau region. Other central Californian nations included the Patwin, Miwok, Maidus, Yokut, and Wintun. They lived closer to the ocean. To the south, additional nations filled in the landscape, including Cahuilla, Fernandeño, Gabrielino, Juaneño, Luiseño, Nicoleño, Serrano, and Tubatulabal. Many of these nations became known as Mission Indians once the Spanish missionaries arrived in the region, establishing many Catholic missions in the late 1700s.

The earliest Indian occupants of the California region date as early as twelve thousand years ago. These American Indians were big-game hunters who were nomadic. In time, Clovis and Folsom points were used in hunting. For example, by 7000 B.C., one big-game

Many of the American Indians in California today are descended from the Indians that lived there before the arrival of European settlers. Above, an American Indian dances at the Cal State Long Beach Annual Pow Wow on March 11, 2007.

hunting culture, the San Dieguito culture, used chipped-stone tools and weapons and stone-tipped spears. By 5000 B.C., the population of California was already extensive. The dominant culture was the desert culture. With the large animals extinct, the people gathered seeds and wild plants and used milling stones to grind food. They also hunted and fished.[8]

Between 2000 B.C. and A.D. 500, the Middle Period culture was dominant in California. It featured the use of small canoes and boats to hunt dolphins and other marine animals. These Indians were more sedentary, building villages while remaining nonagricultural. As with other groups, they harvested acorns as a staple food. During the millennium before the arrival of Europeans (A.D. 500–1500), the region experienced great population growth and greater variations of political units. Many nations borrowed culture from the Pacific Northwest, Great Basin, and Plateau tribes. Most of the modern nations were in place by 1300. They were already occupying land they would still be living on when Europeans arrived two centuries later.

In the Northwest

The Pacific Northwest culture group occupies the smallest region of all the tribes of North America. The region includes a long strip of land stretching from the border between modern-day Oregon and California north to the

American Indians of the Pacific Northwest made fish, especially salmon, a large part of their diet.

Alaskan coast. This long expanse of land is never wider than one hundred miles from east to west, hugging the Pacific Coast from beginning to end.

Over the centuries, the tribes found in this region have adapted their culture to fit their environment. Due to the region's high rainfall—typically one hundred inches annually—life in the Pacific Northwest is different from that of any other culture region. It is a land of great forests, coastal waters, and rivers abundant with fish.

95

Chief among the fish was salmon. Just as with the American Indians of the Plateau region, the Indians of the Pacific Northwest relied heavily on these fish that numbered in the millions in the icy waters of the region's lakes and rivers. While salmon was an important freshwater food source, the Pacific Ocean provided another: whales. These great beasts of the ocean provided the Indians with blubber and whale oil. They were hunted in great whaling canoes, often carved from a single giant red cedar tree, a process that might take two or three years to complete. Such whaling canoes might hold a crew of eight or nine men. They used harpoons to spear their prey.

The nations of the Northwest spoke different languages and dialects. Dozens of nations had occupied the region since ancient times. Among those American Indian nations recognized were the Haida and Tlingit, who settled in British Columbia; the Chinook, Coos, Duwamish, Takelma, and Tsimshian, who lived in coastal Oregon and Washington; and the Cowlitz, Clallam, Skagit, and Lumni, who found their homes farther inland in Washington and British Columbia, settling along various rivers.[9]

Dating the earliest arrivals of American Indians to the Northwest region is difficult. Since the early Indians to the region did not use pottery, a traditional means of dating ancient people, archaeologists have relied on various projectile points instead. The earliest occupation in the region, a period called the Coastal Land Hunting period, dates from around 6000 B.C. Hunters used flaked stone-tipped implements of the Clovis variety. It is not until 3000 B.C. that anthropologists and archaeologists again pick up the trail. That culture is known as the Early Maritime, and it was based on the coast. Inhabitants of the Northwest used harpoons to hunt sea mammals, and slate to make their stone projectile points and tools. These practices were similar to those of the Inuit, or Eskimo, who lived farther north in modern-day Canada.[10]

Following the Early Maritime period, anthropologists and archaeologists identify eras of cultural advancement that included new hunting practices both on land and sea. By A.D. 1, the Northwestern cultural practices and values were based on hunting, fishing, and cultivating and gathering wild plants. There was still no systematic agriculture among these peoples. Over the past seven centuries, Northwestern American Indians had developed their intricate social systems and became extraordinary craftsmen. They hewed the various woods of the region into a variety of art forms, tools, and hunting objects—everything from fancy wooden bowls to gigantic canoes measuring sixty feet in length to tall poles, called totem poles, made from fir trees.

American Indians carved and painted totem poles with images of totems. A totem is a natural object, often an animal, taken as a symbol of a tribe, clan, or family.

Totem Poles of the Northwest

Northwest Indians created a unique art form called the totem pole. These poles were typically carved from cedar and served several purposes for their owner, depending on the type of pole. The most common totem pole was the memorial pole, which American Indians erected to note the rise in power of a family member to noble status. Another pole variety, the mortuary pole, was often placed near the grave of a deceased leader. At the top of such poles, a container holding the ashes of a cremated chief might be placed. Yet another type of pole was the potlatch pole, carved to further the prestige of a family after they had hosted a special ceremonial gathering and feast called a potlatch. Another common totem pole was called the house pole. These highly symbolic poles were raised either outside the front door or inside the home

The Symbolic "Life" of a Totem Pole

Totem poles featured a variety of animal-spirit creatures, or totems, that were stacked on top of one another. Such poles might depict Eagle, Killer Whale, Wolf, Raven, the mythical beast Thunderbird, or the monstrous bird, Hokhokw, whose long beak was powerful enough to crush a warrior's skull. Including a particular animal in a totem pole was a way for a wealthy person to pay his respects to the spirit of the animal.

and proclaimed the family's status to all who passed by or entered.[11]

Religion in the Western Region

The religious acts of prayer, experiencing visions, and curing the sick dominated the spiritual lives of many of the American Indians of the Western region. Chief among the religious leaders of many of these tribes were the specially designated spiritualists called shamans. These medicine men bore the responsibility of curing the sick members of the group. Great Basin religion relied heavily on the concept of the spirits, which might influence their lives, as well as a reliance on the powers of shamans and special dances. Not only could shamans heal, but they could also curse. Shaman curses could be cast on a human being, causing physical and mental illness, even delirium.

The supernatural beings found in Northwestern mythology are a combination of both helping spirits and those who do evil or mischief. Men and women called on the spirits to give them blessings in nearly everything they did, from hunting and going to war, to carving a canoe or making a basket. Those seeking help from the gods approached them in a variety of ways, including prayers, incantations, and charms. They also took pilgrimages to sacred places such as lakes, rivers, mountains, and valleys. They also approached their shamans who might serve as go-betweens, since they were seen as the nation's members with the most direct connections to the spirit world.[12]

As for California Indians, their religion included denying themselves certain foods or activities. They also recognized the power of their gods. California Indians also believed that their daily, physical lives could make contact with the spirit world. These American Indians practiced many different ceremonial rituals that helped them mark the passing days of the calendar by recognizing the changing seasons. These nations of Californians believed in a number of gods. Each god had control over a given aspect of a person's life. Californians believed that, through their rituals, they were recognizing the power of their various gods.

A European Arrival

The lives of American Indians in the West, and throughout the Americas, were soon to change. At the end of the fifteenth century, a European explorer arrived with three ships. He, his crew, and the groups of other Europeans that came after him would impact the lives of American Indians forever.

Chapter 8

Winds of Change

Early on the morning of October 12, 1492, European sailors sighted a land they had never seen before. They were part of a Spanish flotilla of only three small wooden ships. They had sailed across the Atlantic Ocean under the sponsorship of Ferdinand and Isabella, the king and queen of the Spanish Empire. Christopher Columbus was the captain of these ships of discovery. Before the end of the day, Columbus and his men would reach the shores of an island in the Bahamas. With their arrival in the Americas, which they called the New World, the history of the world would never be the same.

Ironically, Columbus had not been searching for the lands he landed on. He had been attempting to sail to the west to reach the Far East in Asia, with its valuable spices, silks, hardwoods, and other treasures. During the months that followed his October landing in the Caribbean, he remained convinced he had arrived in what was then called the "Indies." So certain was the Italian sea captain of his success that he called the new people he encountered "Indians."

In 1492, Christopher Columbus lands on an island he named San Salvador, which is located in the Bahamas.

Exploiting New World Peoples

When Christopher Columbus returned to the Caribbean in 1493, he brought a large group of colonists. The small number of colonists he had left behind in 1492 had been killed because the colonists treated the Indians poorly. When Columbus returned that same year, with over one

thousand eager colonists under his command, the Spanish were not guaranteed their efforts would succeed.

The Caribbean Indians fought to remove the unwanted Spanish presence. Then, the well-armed Spanish—with their muskets, armor, dogs, ships, and cannons—put down the Indian attacks, crushing all resistance. The Spanish then controlled most aspects of Indian life, turning them into slaves and forcing them to work in their own mines. They also forced them to pay tribute to the new power in the New World—the Spanish conquistadors, soldiers who were well armed and ready to use their might against a simpler foe.

Everywhere the Spanish went, the pattern was usually the same. In 1519, another Spanish conqueror, Hernán Cortés, invaded the great empire of the Aztecs. With only hundreds of soldiers, as well as thousands of Indian allies, he brought down the empire, killing thousands and destroying the Aztec capital, building by building. In 1539, another Spanish conquistador, Hernando de Soto, governor of Cuba, landed in what is now Tampa Bay, Florida. During a three-year march across the American Southeast, he raided countless American Indian villages and killed all who stood in his path. Over and over, Spanish conquerors left a trail of blood and destruction among their American Indian victims.[1]

The numbers tell the harsh story. Throughout the 1500s, for example, the estimated Mexican Indian population was reduced from 25 million to one million. But war was not the main cause of this destruction. Instead, disease killed most of the Indians. European diseases, introduced mainly through simple contact, laid waste to whole groups of Indians. Smallpox, measles, diphtheria, typhoid, and a list of plagues and fevers ran unchecked through Indian populations. Indians did not have natural immunities to such "new" diseases.

Once smallpox arrived in the Caribbean in 1518, one out of every three Indian people on the island of

Worldwide Food Exchange

A positive aspect of exchange between American Indians and Europeans was food. Colonists discovered and took back to Europe such new foods as the potato, squash, pumpkin, corn, and tomato. American cotton also proved better than Asian types. In return, the New World saw its first lemons, coffee, sugarcane, wheat, oranges, rice, and lettuce. Animals were also exchanged. The horse was introduced to American Indians, as well as cows, chickens, sheep, and pigs. These provided new sources of meat, hides, and wool, changing native cultures forever. New World tobacco became widely used in Europe and other parts of the world. And two great New World tastes also made their way to Europe through vanilla beans and cacao, the substance used to make chocolate.

Hispaniola (present-day Haiti and the Dominican Republic) died within one year. The following year, measles struck, killing even larger numbers than smallpox. Twenty years later, the island's native Taino population numbered only a few thousand. The year before Columbus's arrival on the island, the Taino numbered approximately one million.[2]

During the centuries that followed the arrival of the first Europeans to the New World, American Indian groups continued to struggle. Additional European powers found their way to America—the French, British, Dutch, Portuguese, Swedish—with each establishing colonies on Indian-occupied lands. In some cases, these new European groups found ways to cooperate with American Indians. The French established an extensive empire based on trading furs with the native nations, resulting in a long period of cooperation and mutual benefit. But in most cases, when Europeans arrived to take their place on American soil, it would mean the uprooting of Indian populations. The result was that American Indians typically lost their land, their security, and their cultures were destroyed.

Change became the norm for American Indians between the sixteenth and nineteenth centuries. Sometimes, the changes were positive for the Indians. Certainly, American Indian groups benefited by adopting the horse into their cultures, an animal the Spanish introduced to the Americas. Indians also adopted firearms, as well as metal tools and weapons from the Europeans. While such things might improve American Indian lifestyles, they also changed their cultures. By switching to iron cooking kettles, some American Indians stopped making pottery. By adopting the horse, the people of the Great Plains became more mobile. This led some to nearly abandon farming and to become more reliant on hunting bison. Change for American Indian populations was constant.

With those changes, American Indian culture moved into a new era. The European settlers altered the worlds the Indians had created for themselves, after thousands of years of adapting to life in the Western Hemisphere. What were the achievements of the American Indians prior to the arrival of Columbus and all those who would soon follow him to the New World?

American Indians had established clear political and social systems. In some cases, the leaders were the women, rather than the men. In the Northeast, women served as the heads of individual family units as well as clans. Women also chose which men would be allowed to sit on tribal councils. All this indicates an open-minded approach to leadership practiced by some American Indians prior to the arrival of the Europeans.

By the time of Columbus, Indians lived in nearly independent villages where the needs of all members of

their band, clan, or nation could be met. Some American Indian locations were more than that. They were New World cities where tens of thousands of people lived, worked, played, raised their children, and made lives for themselves. Those Indians who occupied the land of North America in 1492 worked a variety of handicrafts, producing elegant pottery, handmade weapons and tools, ornamental items, and utilitarian wares for cooking, farming, and living.

They had established extensive systems of farming, growing large fields of crops ranging from corn to beans to squash. Indians had established extensive trade routes and had worn down long trails that crisscrossed the various regions of modern-day America. Many of those Indian trails and paths would one day become the routes for modern American roads and highways.

American Indian religions were well defined prior to the arrival of the Europeans. They engaged in long-standing rituals, and forms of worship, including dances, songs, and prayers. The American Indian world of 1492 was a vibrant quilt of different cultures stretching from North to South America. These cultures were typically highly complex and well established. The world of the American Indians was as advanced as any that had ever existed since the arrival of the first human beings in the Western Hemisphere thousands of years earlier.

The Continuing Legacy of the American Indian

Today, the Western Hemisphere is still home to the millions of descendants of American Indians similar to those who greeted the new European arrivals. Even across five hundred years, modern-day American Indians continue to feel the impact of the arrival of Europeans. Throughout the past five centuries, millions of Europeans have found their way to the New World. They built homes, purchased or stole lands from American Indians, and established new societies and nation states.

Throughout those centuries, the original inhabitants of the Americas, the Indians, have struggled to survive. Epidemics of diseases carried by Europeans raged through native towns, killing millions throughout North America. They constantly engaged in warfare with the Europeans, sometimes winning the battles, but rarely winning the wars. Slowly, American Indian cultures were forced to give way to the advance of the newcomers. Treaties were made along the way, especially after the United States was founded. However, Americans often broke these agreements.

Yet the American Indians and their descendants have managed to survive. For many of today's American Indians, their lives are a combination of the old and the

Despite experiencing hardships over hundreds of years, American Indians still celebrate their vibrant cultures today.

new. Almost from the beginning, Europeans expected the Indians to adapt to their presence, to assimilate, or become like the Europeans themselves. Europeans, and their ancestors, including the majority of the residents of the United States, believed their cultures were superior to those of the American Indians. After all, they had guns and large ships; they had special skills and their favored crops and livestock. They believed they had a better religion, Christianity. The new arrivals to the New World were determined from the outset to turn the New World into their world. American Indians were often forced to adapt or perish.[3]

Indeed, American Indians did learn many of the ways of the Europeans. Indians eventually understood the concept of private individuals owning pieces of land. They changed their clothing styles, learned to eat new foods, became skilled in European and, later, American crafts and other skills. Many converted to Christianity. Throughout the centuries, they would become farmers, ranchers, blacksmiths, soldiers, shopkeepers, sailors, ironworkers, factory workers, and office workers.

But many modern-day American Indians still retain aspects of their ancestors' ways of life. Across the American Southwest, Pueblo Indians live in adobe and stone houses that their ancestors built centuries ago, even as their windows have glass and the furniture inside their homes was bought at Sears. Outside their

ancient adobes, they park their cars and trucks. To the north, in Alaskan waters, modern-day Inuit still fish in the same waterways their people have for more than a thousand years, although their boats travel those waters using outboard motors.

The lives of many of the American Indians of the twenty-first century continue to straddle two worlds—the modern and the traditional. Although they have changed, having altered many aspects of their daily lives, they continue to keep one foot firmly planted in the past. That past, those long-lost eras of time and space, when their earliest ancestors hunted the lands with stone-tipped spears, fished ancient waters, prayed to their eternal gods of the Sun and the Moon, planted their maize, and formed whole societies based on family, remain a never-changing source of pride for today's American Indians.

TIMELINE

1.8 million B.C.—Ice Age period known as the Pleistocene Era begins. (It ends about 10,000 B.C.) During that era, humans may have reached the New World.

25,000 B.C.—Humans may have reached the Yukon in western Canada, according to evidence found at the "Old Crow" site.

15,000 B.C.—Earliest claim of humans in the United States based on evidence found at the Meadowcroft rockshelter site in Pennsylvania.

12,000 B.C.—Prior to this date, the first migration of people to the Americas takes place.

10,000–13,000 B.C.—Early humans reach the Americas by crossing land bridge called Beringia

10,000 B.C.—Pleistocene Era ends; Neolithic Era begins; Clovis points are used by ancient hunters.

9000 B.C.—Humans arrive in the eastern portion of what later became the United States; earliest inhabitants of the Southwest arrive.

7000 B.C.—Early humans may have reached the southern tip of South America; Mexican Indians are engaging in agriculture.

5000–2000 B.C.—More migrants arrive in North America; they will come to be known as the Inuit.

2500 B.C.—American Indians of the Southwest begin growing maize.

1000 B.C.—Village life established in Mexico.

100 B.C.—Southwestern people are making early forms of pottery; Anasazi culture begins to take shape.

1000 B.C.–A.D. 500—Early Woodland stage: American Indians of the Northeast build earthen mounds.

A.D. 300–900—Peak period for Mayan culture in Central America.

700–1100—The Developmental Pueblo period, the third phase of Anasazi culture, witnesses the building of elaborate, multistoried pueblos.

1100–1400—Peak period for the culture of the Mogollon and Hohokam in the Southwest.

1200—Anasazi culture at Mesa Verde reaches its high point.

1492—Christopher Columbus ushers in the arrival of Europeans into the New World.

1500—The vast majority of American Indian nations have been established and continue into modern times.

1996—Discovery of Kennewick Man's bones along the Columbia River.

CHAPTER NOTES

Chapter 1. An Ancient Hunter

1. James C. Chatters, "Kennewick Man," *Northern Clans, Northern Traces: Journeys in the Ancient Circumpolar World*, 2004, <http://www.mnh.si.edu/arctic/html/kennewick_man.html> (September 18, 2007).

2. Ibid.

3. Ibid.

4. Ibid.

5. Ibid.

6. Michael Lemonick and Andrea Dorfman, "Who Were the First Americans?" *Time*, March 13, 2006, pp. 44–52.

7. Jeffrey Kluger, "Who Should Own the Bones?" *Time*, March 6, 2006, pp. 50–51; J. M. Adovasio with Jake Page, *The First Americans: In Pursuit of Archaeology's Greatest Mystery* (New York: Random House, 2002), p. 247.

8. Adovasio, p. 248.

9. Associated Press, "Appeals Court Says Scientists Can Study Kennewick Man," *Kennewick Man Virtual Interpretive Center*, February 4, 2004, <http://www.kennewick-man.com/kman/news/story/4704603p-4655534c.html> (September 18, 2007).

10. Lemonick, p. 47.

11. Ibid., p. 50.

12. Ibid., p. 48.

13. Ibid.

Chapter 2. America's First People

1. J. M. Adovasio with Jake Page, *The First Americans: In Pursuit of Archaeology's Greatest Mystery* (New York: Random House, 2002), pp. 46–51.

2. Ibid., pp. 45–47.

3. Arrell Morgan Gibson, *The American Indian: Prehistory to the Present* (Lexington, Mass.: D.C. Heath and Company, 1980), p. 10.

4. Jake Page, *In the Hands of the Great Spirit: The 20,000 Year History of American Indians* (New York: Free Press, 2003), p. 19.

5. Ibid., pp. 36–38.

6. Carl Waldman, *Atlas of the North American Indian* (New York: Facts on File Publications, 1985), p. 1.

7. Alvin M. Josephy, Jr., *The Indian Heritage of America* (Boston: Houghton Mifflin Company, 1991), p. 37.

8. Michael Lemonick and Andrea Dorfman, "Who Were the First Americans?" *Time*, March 13, 2006, p. 48.

9. Ibid., p. 25.

10. Hugh Thomas, *A History of the World* (New York: Harper & Row, Publishers, 1979), p. 11.

11. Josephy, p. 271.

12. Ibid., p. 83.

13. Adovasio, p. 157.

14. Brian M. Fagan, *Ancient North America: The Archaeology of a Continent* (New York: Thames and Hudson, 2005), pp. 114, 117.

Chapter 3. Finding Ways to Survive

1. Jake Page, *In the Hands of the Great Spirit: The 20,000 Year History of American Indians* (New York: Free Press, 2003), p. 37; David J. Meltzer, *Search for the First Americans* (Washington, D.C.: Smithsonian Books, 1993), p. 12.

2. "What Is a Sabertooth?" *Univeristy of California Museum of Paleontology*, n.d., <http://www.ucmp.berkeley.edu/mammal/carnivora/saber tooth.htm> (November 5, 2007).

3. Charles C. Mann, *1491: New Revelations of the Americas Before Columbus* (New York: Vintage Books, 2006), pp. 167–170; Page, pp. 22–23.

4. Arrell Morgan Gibson, *The American Indian: Prehistory to the Present* (Lexington, Mass.: D.C. Heath and Company, 1980), pp. 85–86; James Kirby Martin, et al. *America and Its People* (New York: Harper Collins, 1993), p. 11.

5. "Farming," *Book Rags*, n.d., <http://www.book rags.com/research/farming-ansc-02/#bro_copy> (November 5, 2007).

6. Peter Charles Hoffer, *The Brave New World: A History of Early America* (Boston: Houghton Mifflin Company, 2000), p. 38.

Chapter 4. People of the Southwest

1. Alvin M. Josephy, Jr., *The Indian Heritage of America* (Boston: Houghton Mifflin Company, 1991), p. 147.

2. Ibid., p. 152.

3. Juan Schobinger, *The First Americans* (Grand Rapids, Mich.: W. B. Eerdman's Publishing Company, 1994), pp. 60–61.

4. Ibid.; Jake Page, *In the Hands of the Great Spirit: The 20,000 Year History of American Indians* (New York: Free Press, 2003), p. 73.

5. Page, pp. 73–75.

6. Alvin M. Josephy, Jr., *500 Nations: An Illustrated History of North American Indians* (New York: Gramercy Books, 1994), p. 56.

7. Josephy, *Indian Heritage*, p. 156.

8. Brian M. Fagan, *Ancient North America: The Archaeology of a Continent* (New York: Thames and Hudson, 1991), pp. 136, 181.

9. Josephy, *Indian Heritage*, p. 157.

10. Ibid., pp. 158–159.

11. Josephy, *500 Nations*, p. 58.

12. Ibid.

13. Ibid., p. 57.

14. Josephy, *Indian Heritage*, pp. 158–159.

15. Josephy, *500 Nations*, p. 61.

16. Barry M. Pritzker, *A Native American Encyclopedia: History, Culture, and Peoples* (New York: Oxford University Press, 2000), pp. 5, 33; Arrell Morgan Gibson, *The American Indian: Prehistory to the Present* (Lexington, Mass.: D.C. Heath and Company, 1980), p. 75.

Chapter 5. The Mound Builders and the Iroqouis

1. Alvin M. Josephy, Jr., *The Indian Heritage of America* (Boston: Houghton Mifflin Company, 1991), pp. 83–86.

2. Ibid., pp. 86–87.

3. Ibid., pp. 89, 92.

4. Nancy Bonvillain, *Native Nations: Cultures and Histories of Native North America* (Upper Saddle River, N.J.: Prentice-Hall, 2001), p. 37; Barry M. Pritzker, *A Native American Encyclopedia: History, Culture, and Peoples* (New York: Oxford University Press, 2000), p. 399.

5. Josephy, p. 103.

6. Alice Beck Kehoe, *North American Indians: A Comprehensive Account* (Upper Saddle River, N.J.: Pearson, 2006), p. 160.

7. Ibid., pp. 160–162.

8. Josephy, p. 106.

9. Pritzker, pp. 400, 438.

10. Joy Hakim, *The First Americans* (New York: Oxford University Press, 1993), p. 51.

11. Josephy, p. 92; Jake Page, *In the Hands of the Great Spirit: The 20,000 Year History of American Indians* (New York: Free Press, 2003), pp. 166–167.

12. Arrell Morgan Gibson, *The American Indian: Prehistory to the Present* (Lexington, Mass.: D.C. Heath and Company, 1980), p. 66.

13. Page, p. 164.

14. Pritzker, pp. 437–438, 449, 467.

Chapter 6. Hunting on the Great Plains

1. Barry M. Pritzker, *A Native American Encyclopedia: History, Culture, and Peoples* (New York: Oxford University Press, 2000), p. 291.

2. Alvin M. Josephy, Jr., *The Indian Heritage of America* (Boston: Houghton Mifflin Company, 1991), p. 111.

3. Ibid., pp. 111–112.

4. Ibid., p. 112.

5. Ibid., p. 113.

6. Ibid.

7. Ibid., p. 114.

8. Nancy Bonvillain, *Native Nations: Cultures and Histories of Native North America* (Upper Saddle River, N.J.: Prentice-Hall, 2001), pp. 182–183.

9. Ibid.

10. Arrell Morgan Gibson, *The American Indian: Prehistory to the Present* (Lexington, Mass.: D.C. Heath and Company, 1980), p. 244; Pritzker, p. 294.

11. Pritzker, p. 293.

12. Gibson, p. 244; Pritzker, pp. 293, 298.

13. Pritzker, pp. 293, 298.

Chapter 7. American Indians in the West

1. Alvin M. Josephy, Jr., *The Indian Heritage of America* (Boston: Houghton Mifflin Company, 1991), p. 125.

2. Arrell Morgan Gibson, *The American Indian:*

Prehistory to the Present (Lexington, Mass.: D.C. Heath and Company, 1980), pp. 20–21; Barry M. Pritzker, *A Native American Encyclopedia: History, Culture, and Peoples* (New York: Oxford University Press, 2000), p. 220.

3. Josephy, p. 127.

4. Brian M. Fagan, *Ancient North America: The Archaeology of a Continent* (New York: Thames and Hudson, 1991), pp. 260–261, 304.

5. Pritzker, p. 249.

6. Alice Beck Kehoe, *North American Indians: A Comprehensive Account* (Upper Saddle River, N.J.: Pearson, 2006), pp. 355–356.

7. Josephy, p. 138.

8. Ibid., pp. 139–140.

9. Ibid., pp. 73–74.

10. Ibid., p. 74.

11. Gibson, pp. 84–85; Pritzker, p. 164.

12. Gibson, p. 85; Pritzker, pp. 163–164.

Chapter 8. Winds of Change

1. Peter Charles Hoffer, *The Brave New World: A History of Early America* (Boston: Houghton Mifflin Company, 2000), pp. 85–87, 89; David J. Meltzer, *Search for the First Americans* (Washington, D.C.: Smithsonian Books, 1993), pp. 8–9.

2. Ibid., p. 84.

3. Arrell Morgan Gibson, *The American Indian: Prehistory to the Present* (Lexington, Mass.: D.C. Heath and Company, 1980), p. 237, 270; Hoffer, p. 2.

GLOSSARY

anthropologist—Scientist who studies the cultures of humans, both contemporary and ancient.

archaeologist—Scientist who studies historical remains and sites.

assimilation—Adapting or changing one's culture while taking on the culture of another group.

atlatl—Archaic, handheld spear-throwing device designed to increase the velocity and control of a spear.

Beringia—Temporary land bridge spanning the modern-day Bering Strait during prehistoric ice ages.

Clovis point—Stone projectile point used by primitive hunters from 11,500 to 10,000 B.C.

ice age—Geological period of time when a large percentage of the earth's water was locked in ice, causing a lowering of the oceans and seas worldwide.

kiva—A circular chamber built partly underground by ancient Southwest Indians and used for ceremonial and religious purposes.

mastodon—Larger than modern-day elephants, mastodons were similar to, but genetically distinct from mammoths. They lived from 4 million B.C. until they became extinct around 10,000 B.C. They are known for long, curving sets of tusks.

matrilineal—System of identifying a child's ancestry through the mother, rather than the father.

The Native American Graves Protection and Repatriation Act (NAGPRA)—A federal act designed to protect American Indian remains, grave sites, and artifacts.

Neolithic Age—An era following the Paleolithic Age, from approximately 10,000 B.C. until the rise of the Bronze Age, around 3500 B.C.

Paleolithic Age—An era lasting from 2 million years ago until the rise of systematic agriculture between 10,000 and 7000 B.C.

paleontologist—Scientist who studies prehistoric plant and animal life.

Pleistocene Era—Lengthy geological period extending from 1.8 million years ago to approximately 10,000 B.C.

radiocarbon dating—Scientific method used to date artifacts, as well as animal and human remains by measuring the decay rate of the C-14 isotope in organic, carbon-based material such as hair, fur, bone, and plants. The method is fairly accurate for material up to sixty thousand years old.

rockshelter—Natural overhang of rock along a cliff wall that provided shelter for early human beings from the natural elements.

Three Sisters—Refers to the three primary crops raised by many early Indian agriculturalists: corn, beans, and squash.

woolly mammoth—Species of mammal known to have lived from one hundred fifty thousand years ago until it became extinct around 10,000 B.C., at the end of the Pleistocene Era.

FURTHER READING

Books

Crow, Joseph Medicine. *Counting Coup: becoming a Crow Chief on the Reservation and Beyond.* Washington, D.C.: National Geographic, 2006.

Freedman, Russell. *Who Was First?: Discovering the Americas.* New York: Clarion Books, 2007.

Keoke, Emory Dean, and Kay Marie Porterfield. *Encyclopedia of American Indian Contributions to the World: 15,000 Years of Inventions and Innovations.* New York: Facts on File, 2001.

Lauber, Patricia. *Who Came First?: New Clues to Prehistoric Americans.* Washington, D.C.: National Geographic Society, 2003.

Marrin, Albert. *Saving the Buffalo.* New York: Scholastic Nonfiction, 2006.

Sonneborn, Liz. *Chronology of American Indian History.* New York: Facts On File, 2007.

Wood, Marion and Brian Williams. *Ancient America.* New York: Facts on File, Inc., 2003.

Internet Addresses

NPS.gov: Mesa Verde
<http://www.nps.gov/meve/>

Yukon Beringia Interpretive Center
<http://www.beringia.com/>

Index

A

Adena culture, 56, 58
agriculture
    Anasazi, 44, 50
    development of, 36–37
    Great Basin culture, 87
    Haudenosaunee, 63,
      65–67
    Mississippian, 58
    Mogollon/Hohokam,
      41–42
    Natchez, 62
    Pacific Northwest, 97
    Plains Indians, 74, 75,
      76
    Pueblo peoples, 53
Algonquian, 38, 64, 65, 66,
    67
Anasazi, 41
    agriculture, 44, 50
    beginnings, 42, 44
    decline, 50–51
    hunter-gatherer lifestyle,
      44
    spiritual life, 45, 46, 47
animals
    domestication of, 44
    exchange, 62, 72, 105
    of the Pleistocene,
      24–26, 72
Apache, 38, 51, 52
Archaic culture, 55–56
Athabascan, 50–51
Aztecs, 61, 104

B

basket weaving, 52–53, 86
Beringia, 23, 25, 28, 30, 35
bison, 24, 32–33, 72, 74–75,
    107

C

Cahokia, 58–60
calendars, lunar, 62
California culture region, 90,
    92, 94, 101
canoes, 55, 94, 96, 97, 100
catlinite, 83–84
Cayuse, 39, 90
Chaco Canyon, 46–47, 48,
    49, 50
Chatters, Jim, 10, 12–13, 17
Cherokee, 38, 63
Cheyenne, 38, 80
Chickasaw, 38, 63
Chinook, 39, 90, 96
Choctaw, 38, 63
Clovis points, 35, 55, 92, 97
Columbus, Christopher, 102,
    103, 106, 107
corn, 37, 41, 44, 58, 63, 67,
    74, 76, 105, 108. *See also*
    maize.
Cortés, Hernán, 104
counting coup, 80–81
Creek, 38, 63
cultural regions, 37–39

D

Developmental Pueblo
    period, 44–50